CHILDREN'S LITEF

Texts and Contexts
Series Editors: Gail Ashton and Fiona McCulloch

Texts and Contexts is a series of clear, concise and accessible introductions to key literary fields and concepts. The series provides the literary, critical, historical context for texts and authors in a specific literary area in a way that introduces a range of work in the field and enables further independent study and reading.

CHILDREN'S LITERATURE IN CONTEXT

FIONA McCULLOCH

continuum

Continuum International Publishing Group

The Tower Building	80 Maiden Lane
11 York Road	Suite 704
London SE1 7NX	New York, NY 10038

British Library Cataloguing-in-Publication Data
A catalogue record for this book is available from the British Library.

ISBN: 978-1-8470-64868 (hardback)
978-1-8470-64875 (paperback)

Library of Congress Cataloguing-in-Publication Data
A catalogue record for this book is available from the Library of Congress.

Typeset by Newgen Imaging Systems Pvt Ltd, Chennai, India
Printed and bound in India

CONTENTS

ACKNOWLEDGEMENTS

Special thanks to Anna Fleming and Colleen Coalter for their support and commitment to this series; Gail Ashton for her helpful comments, professional outlook, and fabulous friendship; my students, particularly at MMU Cheshire and Bradford University, for their enthusiastic seminar discussions; and, most of all, to Heather Price, for everything.

SERIES EDITOR'S PREFACE

Texts and Contexts offers clear and accessible introductions to key literary fields. Each book in the series outlines major historical, social, cultural and literary contexts that impact upon its specified area. It engages contemporary responses to selected texts and authors through a variety of exemplary close readings, by exploring the ideas of seminal theorists and/or a range of critical approaches, as well as examining adaptations and afterlives. Readers are encouraged to make connections and ground further independent study through 'Review, Reading and Research' sections at the end of each chapter which offer selected bibliographies, web resources, open and closed questions, discussion topics and pointers for extended research.

PART ONE

CONTEXTS

CHAPTER ONE

SOCIAL AND CULTURAL CONTEXT

GROWING PAINS

Childhood is a vague term and notoriously fluid regarding when it ends, dependant upon the historical period in which it is being addressed. It is also a concept that differs geographically and culturally. As such, 'we need to distinguish between children as human beings and childhood as a shifting set of ideas' (Cunningham 2005 [1995]: 1). Thus, '"child" and "childhood" will be understood in different ways in different societies', so, while '[t]oday in the West we do indeed generally associate childhood with such characteristics as innocence, vulnerability and asexuality', on the other hand 'people in, say, the slums of Latin America or a war-torn region of Africa, will probably not do so' (Heywood 2001: 4). Further, there is a paradox: biologically, childhood ends at the onset of puberty with the beginning of adolescence. Historically, one was a physically a child for longer three hundred years ago than one is today. In the eighteenth century, for example, the average age of a girl's onset of menstruation was 16, whereas today that onset is several years earlier. Culturally, however, childhood was significantly briefer in the eighteenth century because many children had to work in factories and picked up on adult attitudes that contemporary children would not be exposed to at such an early age. The majority of children in the 1700s were exposed to more birth, death and sexuality, given that houses had only one or two rooms. Likewise, until 1871, the age of consent was 12 years old. It is generally agreed that the concept of childhood was introduced around the eighteenth century. Prior to this, children were considered to be 'little adults', lacking in grown-up intellect and strength but, nevertheless, undifferentiated in treatment from their adult contemporaries, even wearing smaller versions of the same clothes worn by adults. In terms of parenting, the emphasis was upon obedience and punishment and instilling the values laid down by adults until youngsters became adults. In medieval Britain, it is estimated that the child mortality rate was around one in four failing to reach their first birthday. With this in mind, it is perhaps unsurprising that our modern associations with childhood did not exist in the Middle Ages, as one's child years were fraught primarily with the anxiety of surviving into adulthood. Philippe Aries in *Centuries of Childhood* (1962) believed that 'in medieval society the idea of childhood did not exist' (Aries 1973: 125).

However, that is not to say, argues Cunningham, that the child was not a focus of philosophical debate in the medieval period and there is certainly evidence of societal intervention regarding child-rearing. Part of the shift in attitudes to children came in the move away from paganism, where children apparently were regarded as peripheral, to an emerging Christian culture that gradually centred the child as the focal point of family life. Baptism became a pivotal tool in associating the child with innocence, insofar as the ceremony involves a cleansing of human sin. Depictions of the infant Jesus with the Madonna increasingly generated an iconography of associations between child and mother, with connotations of the child being Christ-like. Thus, this imagery offered 'an ideal of childhood that had considerable sway in the Middle Ages, certainly from the twelfth century onwards' (Cunningham 2006: 28). But a discrepancy arose between the artistic representation and the lived experience of children, who were often the victims of parental violence, neglect or ignorance. In terms of discipline, there was the familiar sentiment that children were becoming increasingly misbehaved and that the only way to maintain obedience was for their parents to chastise them and to instil in them the manners expected by society. So books that were produced with children in mind were for the instruction of parents on how to rear their children in a satisfactory manner. Of course, large sections of the population were illiterate and, consequently, these books were aimed at the more privileged sectors of society. In terms of historical evidence relating to childhood (as with other marginal groups, such as women or the lower classes), it is restricted to what is written *about* them rather than produced by them and is often limited, given the ways in which such marginal groups are written out of history at the expense of those considered to be more worthy. Another difficulty is that much of the evidence gleaned about historical childhood is derived from fictional texts. The relationship between children's literature and childhood, then, is utterly inseparable and somewhere in between these two spaces, real children exist. Heywood confirms that '[s]tudies of the representation of childhood also have a solid base in the literary and visual texts available to them' (Heywood 2001: 6). This is heightened when trying to unearth early historical evidence, for '[m]edievalists face these problems in a particularly acute form' (Heywood 2001: 6). Because of this, 'They risk gaining a seriously distorted impression of ideas on childhood at this early period because they are forced to rely on a small number of texts, many of them fictional in character' (Heywood 2001: 6).

According to Cunningham, there is also evidence of childhood play that is not so different from our contemporary understanding of play. It was based around the seasonal cycle: so, for instance, in autumn orchards were raided by boys or in winter pigs' bladders were used for games of football (Cunningham 2006: 44). The role of girls participating in play is less evident, though undoubtedly had more of a domestic basis, with an emphasis placed upon the importance of maintaining chastity, humility and deference. Likewise, girls were less educated and tended to be illiterate by comparison with boys. Local benefactors tended to provide any schooling that was available in England – again, mainly for boys – but in Scotland there was more of a state involvement, albeit predominantly for the privileged. On the rare occasions when girls were educated, it would often be restricted to reading English rather than any progression to Latin. So it is clear that both female and poor children suffered from lack of educational resources. With the Statute of Labourers 1405–06, they were 'free to set their Son or Daughter to take Learning at any manner school that pleaseth them within the Realm' (Cunningham 2006: 56). But the reality was much less straightforward, with the practicalities of securing an education proving a continuing burden.

SUFFER THE LITTLE CHILDREN

During the Reformation, British society shifted from Catholicism as the establishment of Protestantism became secured with the

'Glorious Revolution' of 1688–89. This included the Church of England, the Puritans in England and Wales, and the Presbyterians in Scotland, the latter's vehement rejection of popery led by John Knox. These religious and cultural shifts, then, had an impact on the attitudes towards children, who were seen as an important ideological vessel in the influencing of the population away from previous Catholic beliefs: the younger one was indoctrinated with the new cultural turn, the more successful would be the indoctrination's embedding in society. Perhaps the main difference in terms of childhood involved a fundamental shift in the way in which children were associated with sin. According to Catholic belief, an infant leaves humanity's original sin behind at the moment of baptism and is thereafter regarded as innocent; for Protestants, this ceremony did not offer such guarantees. Religious instruction, then, became paramount and required parents directly rather than priests to instil in the child a sense of its sin and need for repentance. As head of the family, as king was head of country and God of humanity, the father was expected to discipline his children in accordance with the conduct books produced for him. The emphasis was on it being the father's duty not to 'spare the rod and spoil the child', though this was regarded as being necessary only if verbal discussion failed. William Gouge, a seventeenth-century Puritan minister, wrote in 'A Prayer for a Childe to Use' (1634) that children should regard parents 'as Gods to their children': any disobedience towards a parent was regarded as disobedience to their heavenly Father. Gouge produced its companion 'A Prayer for Parents to Use' (1634; in Cunningham 2006: 67), instructing fathers particularly to undertake their children's provision and training, especially in teaching them biblical doctrine. With child mortality rates so high, it was paramount that parents saved their children's souls; they could never be regarded as too young to receive religious instruction, because at any moment they might have to meet their Maker, so they must be prepared. When they did survive, children had very few rights or status. The view of children, for instance in Calvinist Scotland in the seventeenth century, was that they were nearer to the fall of humanity and, consequently, morally inferior to adults. As such, the sooner they grew up, the better and, until then, any signs of sin should be beaten out of them, even in the richer families.

Depending on social class, boys received some education, often initially attending a dame school – for young children, run by a woman, often in her own home – and then perhaps onto further schooling thereafter. Apart from the affluent classes, boys had to balance education with work in order to support the family income. Boys from wealthier families could attend grammar school but would not go beyond this to university, the latter being the reserve of the privileged classes. Instead, boys tended to seek apprenticeships from about age 14 and in 1562 The Statute of Artificers introduced a compulsory seven-year apprenticeship for those who wanted to become craftsmen or tradesmen. Grammar schools increased, though were often detested by the boys attending them as places of strict punishment; but, again, they were not open to the poor. Girls in the seventeenth century, on the other hand, were restricted in their education on the grounds of gender inequality. This was a step backwards from the Tudors in the sixteenth century, whose more progressive ideas had been influenced by the Renaissance movement spreading from Italy. Sir Thomas More's *Utopia* (1515/16) believed in a state education for both sexes, while in 1559 Thomas Becon questioned why, if 'the youth of the male kind' had access to schooling, then why not also 'for the godly institution and virtuous upbringing of the youth of the female kind?' (Cunningham 2006: 87). But even in the sixteenth century, this was limited, depending on a girl's family attitudes and wealth. So the minority of girls received a good education, while the rest in both the sixteenth and seventeenth centuries were taught at home or placed in service in another household and the end goal was always marriage. Becon wrote, 'A maid should be seen, and not heard', and this was very much a continuum from the Middle Ages, by which time females were regarded as being potential seductresses and corrupters of men, with the reminder of Eve ever present. It was thought that the pursuit of learning and wisdom in women, then, needed to be curtailed for these were believed to lead to dangerous passions; the emphasis was to raise girls to be compliant and passive and to be ever-vigilant lest they show signs of their sinful Mother Eve (Cunningham 2006: 89).

In the mid-sixteenth century, an increase in vagrancy and begging among the populace, including children, caused concern and fear among the authorities. In 1547, the Vagrancy Act granted the removal of such children between the ages of 5 and 14 from their parents by anyone who could occupy them up to age 20 for women and 24 for men, and should they run away, their new guardian could 'use him or her as his slave in all points until it came of age', although the enslavement part of the legislation was repealed two years later (Cunningham 2006: 95). Keeping children occupied seems to be the biggest concern, for in 1536 the Act For Punishment of Sturdy Vagabonds and Beggars granted public authorities the right to remove healthy beggars aged 5 to 14 and 'apprentice them to masters in husbandry or other crafts' (Cunningham 2006: 95). In 1626, the Orders for the Poor said, 'That no child be suffered to beg but that all the children of the poor that are not able to relieve them be set to sewing, knitting, bonelace-making, spinning of woollen or linen yarn, pin-making, card-making, spooling, button-making, or some other handiwork as soon as ever they be capable of instruction to learn the same.' Parliament continued to pass laws affecting poor children, with the 1597 Act for the Relief of the Poor and in 1601 when that act was changed slightly. These acts of intervention affected numerous children from the late sixteenth century until 1834, when it was amended again and was known as 'the Old Poor Law'. The stipulations remained pretty much the same: church-wardens and overseers of the poor in each parish were required to apprentice out not only beggars but any child whose parents were not deemed capable of supporting them financially. A similar act was passed in Scotland in 1572, though it was harder to enforce, given a lack of national and local communication (Cunningham 2006: 96). With the expansion of the British Empire, there was a further response to the burden of poor children on the state: according to one account in 1627, 'There are many ships now going to Virginia, and with them, some 1400 or 1500 children' (Cunningham 2006: 98). Though some parents and their children opposed such exodus, their pleas were ignored and many of the exiled children did not survive the journey.

COMING OF AGE?

By the mid to late eighteenth century, childhood underwent something of a revolution. One of the seventeenth century's most influential philosophers was John Locke, whose *Some Thoughts Concerning Education* was published at the end of the seventeenth century in 1693. Rather than seeing the child as being full of original sin, Locke regarded each child as being born with a 'blank sheet'. The child, then, observed Locke, only has potential and is moulded by its environment, including parents, peers and education. Later, Jeremy Bentham and Robert Owen drew on Locke in emphasizing the importance of the environment to which a child is subjected. Locke believed that there should be more books written for children and starting around 1740 there was a significant increase in the publication of children's books. This was a cultural turn that recognized the importance of seeing children as unique beings with their own idiosyncrasies, rather than seeing them as small adults. This led to a rise in the purchase of the increasingly available books and toys for children (toys were available from the medieval period but increased in number and variety from the end of the seventeenth century onwards). With the intervention of Locke, eighteenth-century toys tended to have an educational slant. Arguably, this change was influenced by a lower mortality rate and higher birth rate by the end of the eighteenth century. From 1750 to 1775, the death rate of ruling class children below 5 years old decreased by 30 per cent. Indeed, from 1800 to 1914, children under 15 were never less than one-third of the British population. As such, there was a steadily growing market for book publishers, especially with increases in literacy among all classes. In a society where most children do not survive infancy, then, psychologically, parents do not get too involved emotionally, since 'there was small reward form lavishing time and care on such ephemeral objects as small babies' (Stone 1990 [1977]: 65). However, if the opposite is the case, then they can invest their emotions in the child with more confidence. This is perhaps one reason why parents became more loving and less punitive towards their offspring, resulting in 'the late seventeenth-century revulsion in many quarters against the brutal flogging that had been standard practice earlier, especially in the public grammar schools' (Stone 1990 [1977]: 278). This warmth was coupled with an increasing surveillance of children, with adults in control of recommending, choosing and purchasing toys and books, with an eye towards educational and social development.

Intellectually, there were three main cultural influences impacting childhood during this period: the Enlightenment, Romanticism and Evangelicalism. The Enlightenment was a European phenomenon arising in mid to late eighteenth century and included, for instance, France and Scotland. With an emphasis on the role of reason and progress, it took an optimistic, progressive view of society and regarded children as having great potential for intellectual development. It tended to echo Locke in stressing the role of education and the environment in shaping children's futures. Reason rather than the fear of punishment was stressed, as it was argued that the trust of children could be won by kindness and reason at certain stages in their development. Childhood was viewed positively and youngsters were not preoccupied with sinfulness, particularly as most were religious sceptics during the Enlightenment. Locke recommended *Aesop's Fables* and *Reynard the Fox* and a steering away from the influence of servants with gothic and folk tales. Fearing the corruption of an overactive imagination or the instabilities of metaphorical language, Jean-Jacques Rousseau on the other hand, suggested that reading should be resisted and only recommended *Robinson Crusoe* for its plain realism, rather than escapes into fantasy fiction. Rejecting the emphasis on reason, Rousseau privileged the importance of nature and playful happiness.

Romanticism goes further than the Enlightenment in eradicating the concept of original sin. Instead, it is turned around: according to the Romantic poet William Wordsworth, the 'child is the father of the man'. Being nearer to its time of birth, a child is closer to God and has insights which an adult can learn from because as humans get older they move away from their birth and their maker. In France, Rousseau wrote *Emile: Or on Education*, and shared Enlightenment views of progress, as did Voltaire. The Romantics believed in the intrinsic goodness of children: if they become sinful it is not because they are children but, rather, because their educators have not nurtured and developed their natural goodness. The child was regarded as a seed or young plant that had to be nurtured and this happy state was viewed with painful nostalgia from the adult perspective, which was seen as a shift away from the intimate relationship with nature that only a child has immediate access to: revisiting childhood was the only way to maintain a link with that time. Childhood, then, was taken to harbour a higher level of perception than adulthood and it was only through a return to childhood thoughts that one could rekindle the world of imagination and nature. Such Romantic views influenced art, with children often depicted with their mothers or alone. Autobiography emerged as a preoccupation with self-reflection by looking back to one's childhood to understand the writer's adult position. The adult world, for Romantics like Wordsworth, was regarded as 'the prison-house', where the self is stifled by learning and socialization processes that stemmed from the Evangelicals and the Enlightenment rationalists. Anathema to such thinking was the work of Anna Barbauld and her brother John Aikin in the 1790s, who produced six volumes of *Evenings at Home*, filled with instructive information that sought to advance rationalist thinking about science and natural history rather than spine-chilling tales of Gothic influence. This tussle between those who privileged the imagination and those who revered reason helped to fuel the debate in the 1840s about the rise of children's fairy tales, with writers like Charles Dickens offering *Hard Times* as a stark criticism against the utilitarian rationalist school of 'facts'.

The Evangelical movement had both positive and negative effects on childhood. Evangelicals were prominent in Britain in the late-eighteenth and early-nineteenth centuries and they were keen on morals and biblical teaching. Sunday schools were founded on this premise and by the 1820s the majority of poor children attended such schools at some stage of their childhood. On the negative side, they were rather seventeenth-century Puritan in ethos and, thus, preoccupied with sin. In 1799, the *Evangelical Magazine* encouraged parents to instruct their children that 'they are sinful and polluted creatures'. Charlotte Bronte's *Jane Eyre* describes a harsh, repressive Evangelical household, demonstrating the joyless, repressive side of Evangelicalism. Thomas Arnold, Headmaster of Rugby School, took an old-fashioned view of children and constantly talked about boys as sinners and every offence against school discipline being an offence against God. In an attempt to control any influences that might shape childhood, Evangelicals published many children's books and depicted children as either being very good or very bad. Those who were very bad tended to tell lies and get their come-uppance, whereas the very good, saintly children often rescued the bad ones. Good children were usually seen as too good for this earth and died in the book, often converting the bad child, as well as sometimes parents and other adults. So, unlike the seventeenth century, there are instances of children converting adults. On a positive note, the Evangelicals, while oppressive and preoccupied by sin, nevertheless believed that everyone could be saved. They stressed atonement and Christ's death on the cross for each of us, and no one was regarded as beyond redemption. As such, there was an optimistic element to it, and Evangelicals tended to be humanitarian. For instance, in the nineteenth century, the Earl of Shaftesbury was at the fore of factory reform in removing children from the workplace.

In terms of the nation, Britain became firmly established as a Protestant country after the 'Glorious Revolution' and its citizens regarded themselves more as a unified nation of British people. This was cemented by the Act of Union 1707 whereupon Scotland became united with England, thus forming a stronger sense of British identity. At the time, Britain was also a dominant global power and regarded its children in terms that reflected this new opulence. Acts of charity became more publicly demonstrated, including the opening in 1741 of the Foundling Hospital in London. In 1699 the Society for the Propagation of Christian Knowledge established 'charity schools' for poor children, where instruction was in reading, writing and religion. By 1729, there were 1,419 of these schools with more than 22,000 pupils. Arguably, the incentive was less an interest in helping children than a fear of Catholicism and the desire to maintain Protestantism, with these institutions seen as 'a Fortress and a Frontier Garrison against Popery' (Cunningham 2006: 105). They were also necessary to counteract the ongoing fear of unoccupied children, so charity schools primarily attempted to bring street children under control. As with the Foundling Hospital, the philanthropy behind charity schools was firmly conservative in its discouragement of social mobility: they must learn their place and be kept down. Even so, they generated a 'feel-good factor' as these children were publicly displayed in an annual festival so that the charity could be regarded as an example of British pride. Appearance was all in terms of sentimentalizing the charity cases as public spectacle: even though most of them were the children of poor parents, they were presented as orphans who had been saved by the great British nation (Cunningham 2006: 106–7). The theme of keeping children occupied was continued in the emergence of schools of industry, with even Prime Minister William Pitt expounding in 1796 that '[e]xperience had already shown how much could be done by the industry of children' (cited in Cunningham 2006: 108). John Locke, renowned for his progressive liberal views on childhood, simultaneously regarded poor children as problematic, since '[t]he children of the labouring people are an ordinary burthen to the parish, and are usually maintained in idleness, so that their labour also is generally lost to the public, till they are twelve or fourteen years old' (cited in Cunningham 2006: 108). As part of a select committee on the Poor Laws in 1817 he, thus, recommended that they should 'from their infancy be inured to work, which is of no small consequence to the making them sober and industrious all their lives after' (cited in Cunningham 2006: 109).

The eighteenth century, nevertheless, was a time in which childhood really began to emerge as a distinct cultural identity, a period that is very much responsible for how we see ourselves even today as individuals, and to their privileging of the imagination and nature as central creative forces. It was a time of great social and political upheaval, influenced by the French Revolution, where there was much political agitation in Britain, culminating in fear that Revolution would spread its way across the Channel. It was the period during which William Blake, a Romantic poet who revered childhood innocence, imagination and potential, wrote *Songs of Innocence and of Experience*, and when William Wordsworth's *Preludes* reflected on the golden age of his boyhood, where he was free to roam around an idealized English landscape, believing 'the child was the father of the man'. Nostalgically reflecting on his own childhood, he recognized a relation between this stage and nature, which became a key factor of Romanticism. There is a struggle between Evangelicals, Romantics and rationalists and it is out of this contention that our present day view of childhood is shaped. It is perhaps not surprising that such turbulent times laid the backdrop for the emergence of childhood as a focal point of innocence, where previous debates had seen them as receptacles of original sin and, therefore, in need of instruction. Such instructional thought offered morality reflected in tales like Maria Edgeworth's *Early Lessons* (1801) where the heroine, Rosamond, is taught a series of lessons by her mother, notably an adult figure, in order to show her the error of her ways and set her upon the right path.

IDEALIZED CHILDHOOD

In the nineteenth century, Britain underwent an Industrial Revolution which significantly impacted the role of childhood

and how it was perceived in society. Rapid migration from country to city meant that there were poor living conditions that created numerous social problems. Children had to work under strict
discipline in the factories, prompting reformers and Evangelical
philanthropists to agitate for their removal from such workplaces.
The 1833 Factory Act stipulated that children under 9 were not
allowed to work in factories, while those aged 9 to 13 were limited
to an eight-hour day and were required to have two hours of education a day. Though not without its enforcement problems, this
act set a precedent for the moral argument that children should be
removed from work and, instead, be schooled. It paved the way for
compulsory education first introduced in the 1870 Education Act
(attendance was not compulsory until 1880, though in Scotland
compulsory attendance for children from 5 to 13 years old began
in 1872), whereas up until this point education had been controlled
by religious organizations. Part of the push for state-run schooling came with the Second Reform Act of 1867, which gave suffrage
to most working-class men, so it became important to educate
those with the vote. To maintain Britain's global dominance, it also
became necessary to educate the future workforce and there was
the ongoing fear of children being idle. Education was no longer fit-
ted around a child's working hours but, instead, now took priority,
though working-class parents often resisted this, especially when
it came to keeping their daughters at home to help with domestic
duties. In 1893, the school-leaving age increased from 10 to 11, and
then to 12 in 1899. By the end of the century, children and parents alike accepted that attendance was compulsory and avoidance
would lead to court, though for the poor any prolonged education
was unlikely beyond the compulsory years because of the pressing
need to contribute to the family income. What is also clear, though,
was the disparity of social class conditions for children and the way
that reformers pushed the idea of an idealized childhood as the natural state for all children . Childhood, then, became increasingly
regarded as a separate sphere from adulthood, given the freedom
to be indulged outside the world of work, and it became a cher-
ished time of nostalgia to be protected, as the Victorians inherited
Romantic discourses about childhood innocence. Adults revering memories of their own childhood came to associate childhood
with a rural timeless and better past, so it often became a place of
escapism from the alienating effects of adulthood, which including

the ills of urban life. Thus, the cult of childhood spread with the investment of adults who wished to hold on to that world of care-free innocence as a new Eden in a fallen world. Unlike in the medieval period, when one's adult years were considered the pinnacle of life, the Victorians regarded childhood as the best time and everything beyond as its loss. This childhood divinity was represented in the iconography of paintings by, for instance, John Ruskin and Kate Greenaway. Childhood became a metaphor for the desires of Victorian society and served as a means of alleviating its many fears and anxieties. But this adult fantasy in the representation of childhood was considerably at odds with the reality of those children working in factories or mines or chimneys or elsewhere in Britain's industrial landscape. For James Kincaid, 'One of the most baffling of the many mysteries of Victorian culture is this split between little Oliver Twist in the novel and little Oliver Twist in life', since '[o]ne is fawned over, protected, lusted after; the other is beaten, starved, imprisoned, transported' (Kincaid 1992: 74). In our view of Victorian childhood, it is easy to forget the reality in favour of the representation, since, 'It's just that we are very likely to maunder on about the Wordsworthian child and forget the thundering counter-chorus of carelessness, contempt and abuse' (Kincaid 1992: 74).

Reacting to public fears about industrial urbanization, the new Poor Law of 1834 sought to impose order and control over the working class by enforcing entry to the workhouses, where children were separated from parents and were subject to instruction on the economy and hard work. The emphasis was upon the imposition of facts as was lampooned in Dickens's *Hard Times*. Under the Poor Law, many children in London were relocated to northern England and the Midlands to work in the factories, and the cotton mills thrived on what became known as 'free labour'. By the 1870s, most Victorians felt that the cruelties of child labour had lessened with the passing of legislation, but until then it was certainly a dark period in Britain's history. Many voices advocated the removal of children from the workplace because it was against a child's nature, which was regarded as innocent and playful, and also completely at odds with the image of Britain as a global leader of freedom and cultural perfection. The Society for the Suppression of Juvenile Vagrancy, set up in 1808, became in 1830 the Children's Friend Society, whose aim was 'to rescue from early depravity children who are actually running wild about the streets'. The Victorian period also saw the emergence of 'ragged schools' to instruct Britain's street children (Cunningham 2006: 162). Philanthropists like Thomas Barnardo, a Nonconformist, founded organizations upon denominational lines and a Church of England version was established by Edward Rudolf that is now called The Children's Society. In the 1880s, the National Society for the Prevention of Cruelty to Children (NSPCC) was founded, notably later than the Royal Society for the Prevention of Cruelty to Animals (RSPCA), which emerged in the 1820s. Such provisions led to an increase in cases of child neglect reaching court, with *The Times* reporting 385 cases of child neglect and sexual abuse between 1785 and 1860 (Cunningham 2006: 165). The NSPCC recognized that most abuse and neglect occurred in the home and engineered a nation-wide campaign for public support: by 1910 it had 250 inspectors dealing with more than 50,000 complaints (Cunningham 2006: 165). While attempt was made to prevent family break-up, nevertheless, as with the seventeenth-century transportation of children to the American colonies, Britain's empire became the solution for dealing with child criminals and poor children. Children who had entered the care of Barnardo's or any of the other Poor Law organizations were often shipped to the imperial outposts: the years 1868 to 1925 saw around 80,000 boys and girls (mostly under age 14) sent to Canada to work as agricultural labourers and domestic servants (Cunningham 2006: 166). Apparently, 'so it was across the empire, and there is something unsettling, at the very least, in the image of these droves of little children being shipped off forever to strangers. How precious or how innocent could they be?' (Kincaid 1992: 75).

In terms of gender divisions, there was a glimpse in the 1830s of blurred roles, such as 'knee-length dresses and long white trousers, with hair cut short' being 'recommended for both boys and girls' (Cunningham 2006: 141). However, this was quickly superseded by the growth of public schools from this period into the 1840s when gender divisions were further polarized. Influenced by the Romantic and Evangelical reverence of the relationship between mother and child, the Victorians continued this gender dichotomy. At the same time, employment patterns changed, with the middle-class household becoming ever separate from the world of work. The home, then, became increasingly feminized as a place in which the wife and mother should focus on domesticity. This was the time when separate spheres ideology was most prominent, with men considered suited to the public sphere and women confined to the private sphere. So, unlike Puritan eighteenth-century beliefs that fathers should take control of child-rearing, the father were relieved of this duty, as it was thought that mothers could better meet the child's spiritual needs. Mothers were to keep the home fires burning by nurturing their children and providing a haven of comfort for their husbands to unwind after the toils of public duty. Children became the focus of the feminized family home, with birthdays being annually celebrated and Christmas shifting firmly into childhood territory with the arrival of Santa Claus from America in the 1870s. This domestic environment was considered suitable for both sexes up to about age 6 or 7, but boys were to be removed from this influence thereafter, lest they become effeminate.

This largely explains the rise of public schools as part of the British way of life, as it was expected that all boys of the affluent classes should attend. The prime intention was that boys should learn to become men and, as such, the emphasis was upon physical education and the cultivation of manliness. One of the most famous examples was Thomas Arnold's head mastery of Rugby School in 1828, which inspired Thomas Hughes's *Tom Brown's School Days* (1857). The need for manliness coincided with Britain's dominance as a global empire and the desire that young men represent their race as being the fittest and most deemed to rule inferior nations. The desire for physical prowess also carried with it a hyper-masculinity, which demanded that boys repress their emotions and be stiff-upper-lipped from an early age; hence their removal from the feminine domestic sphere and into the harsh public sphere of public school. Having gained a camaraderie with their peers and an attached loyalty to their school, it comes as little surprise that many who went through this system became confirmed bachelors in their reluctance to return to the feminine home, often choosing, instead, to work in distant outreaches of the empire. Those who did marry often waited until well into their 30s and tended to feel redundant from any domestic role, which, in turn, isolated them from their children. Spaces within the home became masculinized, such as the library or the billiard room (Cunningham 2006: 144–6).

Girls tended to be taught at home by a governess until about age 10, often sharing such lessons with male siblings. If education continued, the girls could attend a local day school for two or three years, followed by a boarding school until about age 17. This generally remained the case until the outbreak of the First World War, with girls often absent from school to help their mother with domestic chores. The purpose of their education was to prepare them for married life; a government inquiry in the 1860s noted that a boy's education was to prepare him for the outside world, while a girl's was for the drawing room. The private schools they attended kept them away from girls of lower social classes and prevented them from discussing politics or reading newspapers. Any newspaper clippings they might read would have to be approved by the patriarch's permission. Several new schools were founded, such as in London or Cheltenham, but they tended to remain conservative in their pedagogical outlook and stemmed from the initiative and ideological control of men. Because of separate schools, gender roles became more widely divided than in any previous historical epoch in Britain. Such division was increasingly challenged by suffragists and other feminists, but this long struggle is arguably still being fought in many ways.

TWENTIETH-CENTURY CHILDHOOD

In 'the century of the child', twentieth-century Britain focused on its future generation as pivotal to the nation's destiny, particularly after two world wars. It became a more child-centred society, with the child's happiness regarded as paramount for good health. However, children were not really considered on an individual basis, but as a collective group issue that urgently needed to be addressed for social well-being. In terms of thinking, behaviourism emphasized obedience and discipline, though from the 1930s this was challenged by a different perspective; still, the weight of concern equated childhood as essential for maintaining Britain's empire and national status, which had begun to be weakened by the wars. As with the Victorian period, the fear was that working-class children might contribute to the degeneracy of the race, a Social Darwinist view inherited from Charles Darwin's theory of evolution and species survival. A stronger link was forged between children and mothers, with the empire being coined 'Mother Empire'. Elementary schools instilled the belief in children that the empire had been built by heroic figures, culminating in the establishment of Empire Day when schoolchildren would celebrate Britain's empire, with the emphasis on its military power. Books, magazines, toys and films that were full of imperial messages supported such propaganda. In 1924, London hosted the British Empire Exhibition. As well as offering inspiring stories of adventure for children to enact heroic fantasies, the empire also served as a solution to social problems: children continued to be transported to the colonies and then the commonwealth into the 1960s. Between 1912 and 1967, some 6,000 children were forcibly emigrated to Australia (in November 2009, Prime Minister Gordon Brown issued an apology to those children who had been exported to the former colonies in the twentieth century).

City-dwelling children, who tended to be working class, became the focus of public health concerns as part of the drive to prevent racial degeneration. A sense of the need to reconnect such children with nature gathered momentum. Margaret McMillan, a pioneer in child welfare and education, opened a city garden in Deptford in an attempt to bring some of the countryside into the urban areas but, ideally, it was argued that city children needed to be removed to the countryside. After much agitation to alleviate some of the hardship endured by children in poverty, particularly in the cities, the family allowance was introduced in 1946. To maintain vigilance on their health, an act introduced in 1907 allowed medical inspection of schoolchildren. Often, too, the fear continued about the dangers of children to society and the need to bring them to heel, so this surveillance further questions just how child-centred such government focus was. Those who had lost parents and found themselves in care homes, such as Barnardo's, felt over disciplined and deprived of ample food or any love, while their individual identities were further eroded by the practice of replacing their names with numbers. However, in 1946 a government committee headed by Dame Myra Curtis reported on the vast number of children in care and the lack of affection shown to them. Following the Curtis Report, the Children Act of 1948 stipulated that every local authority must set up a children's committee to further the best interests of such children. There was a drive to prevent the break-up of the family unit or to encourage fostering, thus signalling the demise of large homes.

The 1902 Education Act expanded the ability of children from elementary schools to continue into secondary education; the 1918 Act increased the school-leaving age to 14; and the 1944 Act raised it to 15, and made attendance at secondary school mandatory at either of the three new types established: grammar schools, secondary modern schools or technical schools. With the coming of the Welfare State, the importance of childhood played an integral part, including the Education Act 1944, the Family Allowances Act 1946 and the Children Act 1948 and the benefits of a National Health Service.

School for girls meant that domestic roles could be reinforced: the nineteenth century introduction of sewing continued along with cooking classes and how to care for babies, known as 'mothercraft'. While the mortality rates for those over the age of one had been steadily declining since the 1850s, nevertheless a quarter of a million under that age died annually. The cause was believed to be hygiene, so mothers were blamed for negligence in this area. Such scientific arguments were also complimented by a rise in psychology relating to child rearing. As though responding to the desire that children be raised in the countryside, with the coming of Second World War, many city children were evacuated, so that in September 1939 826,959 unaccompanied children were evacuated along with 523,670 mothers with pre-school children. Some children thrived on this and were treated well while others were not so lucky and became overworked and underfed. The *Mothercraft Manual* published in 12 editions between 1923 and 1954 noted that 'Self-control, obedience, the recognition of authority, and, later, respect for elders are all the outcome of the first year's training.'

Sigmund Freud famously challenged the view of childhood innocence when he wrote on childhood sexuality, although psychiatrists had written about children's sexual tendencies in the nineteenth century. Freud's views, however, triggered further concern about childhood behaviour, such as bedwetting or thumb sucking because they were now associated with psychosexual problems that required expert intervention. In the late 1920s Child Guidance Clinics sprang up, furthering the shift in emphasis away from behaviourism and the need for discipline to psychology and the focus on childhood anxieties, fears and wishes. Resultantly, there was a move away from corporal punishment, though it was not eradicated in schools until 1982 and it can still occur in the home. This culminated in Dr Spock's *The Common Sense Book of Baby and Child Care* (1946) and a growing insistence on the importance of the mother/child bond, particularly promoted by developmental psychologist Dr John Bowlby. So the first half of the twentieth century involved a struggle between behaviourist and psychologically informed ideas about childhood and the latter won the day. The family became a central focal point of attention in its significance in the shaping of a child's character. Family sizes were generally much smaller than in the nineteenth century, usually with 2 or 3 children, so that by the 1930s demographers feared the decline of the British population due to what was regarded as the failure of women to enact their function as reproducers. Small families, though, tended to mean that children could expect more parental attention than their ancestors received. The home rather than the street became a new childhood space as homes became more comfortable and less overcrowded. This was reflected in developments in radio for children: *Children's Hour* began in 1923 and was described by the BBC's first director-general Sir John Reith as a 'happy alternative to the squalor of the streets and backyards' (Cunningham 2006: 203–4). Hobbies were encouraged like stamp-collecting, model-building and board games as families became clearly more child-centred. Nevertheless, the street still functioned as a leisure space for many children and allowed them to roam largely without adult interference. Another development that attracted children was cinema, although this caused many concerned voices to be raised, but its popularity continued. Boys went more than girls and each week over 4.5 million children visited the cinema. Concerns about how children spent their leisure hours were partly due to fears about adolescence and puberty. Previous centuries had maintained a certain control by apprenticeships or other forms of work, but by the early twentieth century this was filled with education or training. The transition to adulthood through economic status, therefore, was delayed. Adolescence was prolonged and according to American psychologist G. Stanley Hall, lasted up to 25. Youth organizations such as the Boy Scouts were established in 1907 by Robert Baden-Powell, a Boer War hero. The Boys' Brigade was formed in Glasgow in 1883 and was Presbyterian and by the end of the nineteenth century was followed by the Church of England Lads' Brigade, the Jewish Lads' Brigade, the Catholic Boys' Brigade, and the less militaristic Boys' Life Brigade. For girls, there was the Girls' Friendly Society established in the 1870s and in Scotland, from 1900, the Girls' Guildry, while the Girl Guides was formed in 1910. As well as religious foundations, many of these groups were uniformed and ran along militaristic lines. In the 1960s a survey found that one in 3 adults had belonged to the Boy Scouts or Girl Guides, while almost 3 out of 5 men had belonged to a uniformed group as a boy. Clearly there was a drive to provide structure for children and young adolescents rather than leaving them to the dangers of their own devices. But, as voluntary groups, children enjoyed belonging to them. By the mid-twentieth century various spaces competed for children's attention: the street, the home, cinemas and other attractions, and youth organizations.

CONTEMPORARY CHILDHOOD

In the post-war era Conservative Prime Minister Harold Macmillan claimed in 1957, that 'You've never had it so good', referring to the higher standard of living experienced in British society. But the period from the 1970s brought many changes: the employment market became unstable with the decline of manual labour and the so-called feminization of the workforce. The demographics of the nation were altering with more increased immigration, while the face of the nuclear family was altered by a heightened divorce rate. By 1995 over a third of children were born out of wedlock, while in 2005 almost one in 4 children lived in single-parent households, which was a rise of 7% from 1972 (Cunningham 2006: 213). In 1998 the homeless charity Shelter estimated that 100,000 children were homeless at any one time, often because over a third of them lived in families without a full-time wage earner.

While radio and cinema already attracted many children, the appeal of the television spread sharply from the 1950s. Though, historically, children had been expected to contribute to the family economy, from the post-war era this trend was reversed. Instead, the newly coined teenager became a target for market consumption. As well as being able to earn cash, teenagers also benefited from increased parental spending on their behalf. Pocket-money became a factor, with parents often spoiling their children to compensate for their own limited luxuries, particularly among the working class. Often, household chores (which had been an expectation in previous years) could now command money from parents, so that by the 1960s more than half of all 7-year-olds earned money this way. The American historian Viviana Zelizer referred to this new child-centred family life as the 'sacralization of childhood', for it went beyond financial support, as parents invested heavily emotionally and built their aspirations around the success of their children. As well as pocket-money, children were becoming increasingly proficient at pester power, with parents often feeling emotionally blackmailed to fulfil their children's wishes. Communication seemed to increase, too; rather than being seen and not heard, children could now talk more easily to their parents. While things improved, it tended to lead to parental frustrations at disobedience, which were vented by smacking (Cunningham 2006: 215–16).

Childhood became prolonged during this period because the school-leaving age was raised to 16 in 1972. With the changing employment market, children also stayed in the parental home longer, due to economic dependency. As the nuclear family and employment habits changed, children were increasingly expected to help with domestic duties. At the same time, children's rights were being increasingly enforced. From the medieval period to about 1800, children left home about age 14 to earn money, while in the Victorian period teenage workers tended to remain at home, typically only leaving to get married. From the 1970s onwards, it became increasingly difficult to fly the nest, due to financial difficulties. Contemporary society sees a pattern of children often leaving home for university, only to return when they graduate, to be increasingly subsidized by their parents. Childhood as a state of dependency on adults, then, is becoming more blurred. But, while children are increasingly dependent on their parents, they are also now more likely to be contributing to the family income, argues Cunningham (2006). Research in the 1980s and 1990s showed that between a third and a half of those aged 13 to 15 were undertaking some kind of paid employment, such as delivering newspapers, working in shops, hotels, garages and building sites. A proportion of this figure was working more than ten hours a week in addition to their time at school. Children of immigrant communities also often worked. Today, many children act as carers for other family members, including younger siblings and grandparents, with an estimated 175,000 children currently acting as carers. There is a clear paradox between the increasing dependency of children on parents and vice versa, with the latter contributing significantly to the running of the family.

Following the influence of Romanticism where childhood was considered to be a carefree happy period of innocent play, in the

1970s this was extended to include the importance of freedom for individuals to develop their full potential and become healthy adults. This incorporated progressive education, which believed in the innate goodness of children and the discouragement of discipline, and led to the children's liberation movement of the 1960s and early 1970s, though this disappeared with the increasingly difficult economic climate of the 1970s. However, it did leave an influence, as was clear from the 1989 UN Convention on the Rights of the Child. Likewise, Barnardo's no longer encourages children to break contact with their family, but tries to retain links between them. Children now also have rights to bring legal proceedings against their parents in any family disputes (Cunningham 2006: 226). Contemporary society has several tensions: the rights of the child, the obligations felt to the family and economic dependence on the family. Perhaps one of the biggest changes in contemporary childhood has been the use of the street as a place of unsupervised play: the regulation of play areas, the fear of dangers, such as strangers and traffic, and the popularity of television, the internet and multimedia games has all led to a life indoors. The rise in media consumption has generated a vast array of spin-off toys and other merchandise as the child has become increasingly the focus of marketing campaigns, such as the use of packaging and gifts in cereal packs. In 1971, eight out of ten children aged 7 to 8 could go to school alone; by 1991, this had decreased to less than one in ten. In 1982, Neil Postman's *The Disappearance of Childhood* regarded the dominance of new media and visual culture over printed books as a sign that children were becoming levelled with adults, insofar as they can give an instant response rather than have to learn words. If 'learning to read was a difficult task', then 'the visual media required no such prolonged training: everyone, immediately could make some response to a picture' (discussed in Cunningham 2006: 229). Postman contends that the boundary between adulthood and childhood is blurring and is further eroded by the changes in children's clothes, where no clear difference is visible: children are increasingly wearing short versions of adult outfits and adults are often wearing childish gear. So, 'that what was once unambiguously recognized as "children's" clothing has virtually disappeared' (Postman 1994 [1982]: 128). A paradox occurs: children are often more internet-skilled than adults and, therefore, more aware of new media trends in the world. On the other hand, their knowledge of the world has become heavily mediated rather than experienced first hand, given the increasing time spent indoors. All of this has led to a sense that childhood is disappearing, while adults are becoming increasingly child-like in their nostalgic desire to preserve their own youth. Examples include the rise in crossover fiction, such as *Harry Potter* or *His Dark Materials* or the growing adult interest in Playstation or Wii or Nintendo. This group has even been given its own label, known as 'kidults' and are regarded as the most nostalgic generation ever, with constant revivals of music and fashion from the 1980s. Postman (1994 [1982]: 126) alludes to 'the rise of the "adultified" child' concurring with 'the rise of the "childified" adult'.

Rather than placing children in care or shipping them off to the commonwealth, contemporary thinking revolves around maintaining the family. Dysfunctionalism is addressed with the intervention of social workers and various other support networks, but, generally, the dominant view is that the family is the founding fabric of social cohesion. Politicians can constantly be heard talking about 'hard-working families' in their manifestos. Child poverty has remained on the political agenda, but the incidence of children living in poverty has increased from one in ten in 1979 to almost one in three by the late 1990s, which was higher than any other European Union country. While this became a New Labour mission and 700,000 children were deemed to have been 'lifted out of poverty' by 2006, nevertheless New Labour failed to meet their targets, undoubtedly further hindered by the current global recession (Cunningham 2006: 234). A further problem with the family unit is that it is also the site, for some, of utmost danger for a child: according to the NSPCC, in each generation of children, more than 1,000 will be killed at the hands of violent or neglectful parents or carers. In 2001 alone, 65 children in the UK under age 7 died at the hands of parents or carers. This is at the crux of an ideological conflict between those who believe the family is sacrosanct and should be above state intervention, and those who adhere to intervention for the protection of the child. State intervention exposing the Cleveland child sex abuse scandal in the 1980s and in Orkney in the 1990s created a public backlash. Children who had been removed from the family home were returned after claims that parental rights had been thwarted. While in the late-nineteenth and early-twentieth centuries there was much concern about paedophilia in the family home, there has since been 'a convenient silence about the sexual abuse of children in the home' (Cunningham 2006: 237). For much of the twentieth century, the NSPCC and its Scottish wing have instead focused on neglect, mainly in working-class homes. Cleveland and Orkney were the first occasions that sexual abuse in the home reappeared, but the problems with monitoring and proving it were exposed.

With the 1944 Education Act, there was a sense that only a minority of children could pass the 11-plus and attend grammar school, so there was a shift in favour of comprehensive schools, which became the dominant state system by the end of the 1970s. By the late 1970s, 'political commentators' argued that Britain was in decline in relation to its European competitors, both as an economy and state (Cunningham 2006: 237). An education that would suit future entrepreneurs and technicians, while reviving knowledge of the nation's history became a political focus. The national curriculum was introduced in 1988 so that all schools were uniformly structured, while there was a drive to create league tables to measure school performance. Part of this drive included national testing of pupils at set ages of development. As with childhood throughout history, the opinions of children have rarely counted and such educational intervention has pandered to the anxieties and desires of state and parents, alike.

Regarding gender, there is a clear boundary between pink demarcating the girls' area of a toy or clothes shop, while boys have more dark colours. This is now taken as natural, but it is vital to remember that it was as recently as the 1930s that such colour coding was introduced, with blue for boys and pink for girls (Cunningham 2006: 244). It would seem that the historical preoccupation with gender division is still alive and kicking, with only a short recess in the Victorian period when childhood rather than gender was emphasized and boys and girls alike were attired in dresses.

In terms of immigration, Britain has always been multicultural in its formation. Many contemporary children are mixed race and, therefore, often the victims of racist taunts. One of the other contemporary issues has concerned childhood obesity, which has steadily increased, though a report in 2009 suggested that this has now levelled off. Youth crime has been an ongoing public debate throughout history and is currently a hot political topic. In 1963, the Children and Young Persons Act increased the age of criminal responsibility from eight to ten, and court was regarded 'as a last resort for a child committing an offence' (Cunningham 2006: 243). However, from the 1970s, this trend has reversed, as it was felt that punishment rather than rehabilitation was necessary. This sentiment peaked with the 1993 murder of James Bulger by two 10-year-old boys, Robert Thompson and Jon Venables. In 1968, Mary Bell, an 11-year-old child-murderer, was found guilty but press publicity was restrained and the emphasis was on how to rehabilitate her. When Thompson and Venables were convicted, their trial was held in the full glare of media attention and angry mobs awaited them outside court, as they were labelled evil in their childlike amorality. A far cry from Romantic views of innocence. The 1998 Crime and Disorder Act repealed the ancient principle of *doli incapax* (incapable of wrong), whereby a child between age 10 and 13 was deemed incapable of criminality unless proven otherwise by the prosecution. There was now provision for 'Detention and Training Orders' for 'children aged ten and over; 12 year olds could be put into "secure accommodation"' (Cunningham 2006: 243). Cited as a symptom of so-called 'broken Britain' by David Cameron, two unnamed Doncaster brothers aged 10 and 11 were sentenced in January 2010 to a minimum of five years with indeterminate sentences for the brutal attack on two other boys, aged 9 and 11, in April 2009. Michelle Elliot, founder of the charity Kidscape, urged an increased minimum ten years served, arguing that the Doncaster brothers posed a risk to society for many years.

Society has absorbed the Romantic notion of innocent childhood and a child's right to enjoy this happy time dependent on adults, and this happy state is regarded as fundamental to healthy adult development. At the same time, children are expected by adults to behave well and to achieve success along their journey to adult responsibility, as television programmes like *Supernanny* attest. But that happiness can be precarious and undermined by social threats, such as gun and knife crime, sexual predators, drugs, alcohol, family problems, economic downturns and environmental threats like climate change. While children today are not statistically at any greater threat from such predatory deaths as they were previously, nevertheless the perception of danger is much more heightened now. With market consumption driving the pressure to obtain the latest products, the cost of childhood is certainly economically high, but in terms of the cost of happiness and safety, their protection is perhaps even more costly than any financial burden, given the price of their restricted freedom. Children are often associated with the nation in terms of how the future is regarded, as they will always be tomorrow's citizens: just as we fret over the future of the nation, children are a source of constant concern and, therefore, of constant surveillance.

CHAPTER TWO

LITERARY CONTEXT

BEGINNINGS

'Children's literature' is a difficult term to define. Children, in the past and in the present, have read books that were not initially intended for them. So is it fair to say that the term applies only to books written specifically for a child readership, or is the term related to all books that children read? As well as and partly because of this clarity issue, it is virtually impossible to identify the first children's book ever produced. Another difficulty, argues Matthew Grenby (2008), lies in suggesting that children's literature commenced in Britain in the eighteenth century, when there is evidence of children reading fables as far back as ancient Greece, Rome, Egypt, and Sumer. One might make an equally valid case that children's literature emerged in France as much as in Britain. In medieval British society, children were reading fables, courtesy books, journals, ballads, saints' lives, romances and chapbooks, which were short cheap books sold by peddlers.

Children from various classes tended to hear stories too through an oral tradition of storytelling: so, for instance, ruling class children would hear fables told by their servants. Tales, then, were heard by young and old alike and were often bawdy and erotic in content. In medieval society, stories did not exist in the book form that we are familiar with nowadays; instead, they existed as laboriously handwritten manuscripts and would not usually carry an author's name, as stories had often been told and adapted throughout the generations. Stories likely to have been read would have been Geoffrey Chaucer's *Canterbury Tales* (1387) or Aesop's *Fables* or the French *Reynard the Fox*. A literary revolution occurred in the fifteenth century with the advent of the printing press. William Caxton set up Britain's first printing press, upon his arrival in England from Bruges in 1476. Caxton recognized the commercial opportunity this would afford by putting available manuscripts into print, such as *Guy of Warwick*, *The Book of the Knight of the Tower* (1484), *Blanchardyn and Eglantine*, *The Friar and the Boy* and *Aesop's Fables* (1484). Likewise, the fairy tale emerged as a distinctive genre through the appropriation of various oral folk tales involving magic that had been transformed to suit particular societies. This appropriation and transformation of the wonder folk tale or magic tale generally entailed the miraculous transformation of the protagonist from humble origins to greatness. Again, in the fifteenth century the coming of print allowed for much wider dissemination of these wonder tales, which continued through the sixteenth and seventeenth centuries until they evolved into the genre of the literary fairy tale. This literary genre had been derived from the oral tradition of folk tales told by peasants and wonder tales told by all social classes, but adapted to suit aristocratic and bourgeois readers. While they originally tended to be pagan or secular, they became Christianized to fulfil contemporaneous social ideological needs. The fairy tale emerged as a distinctive genre through the appropriation of various oral folk tales involving magic that had been transformed to suit particular societies. So, originally, fairy tales were not written for children and this was the case until into the 1700s (Zipes 1991). In fact, fairy tales belonged to part of an oral tradition in which stories were heard and passed on through generations. Neil Postman argues in *The Disappearance of Childhood* (1982) that the arrival of print culture was crucial to the rise of childhood and this point is echoed by David Rudd who notes that, 'As for childhood itself, it came into prominence with print technology, since which time it has become more and more the focus of consumer interest' (Rudd 2010: 12).

PURITAN INTERVENTIONS

In the sixteenth and seventeenth centuries, Britain shifted away from Catholicism to Protestantism and this brought a fundamental change in the perception of childhood, which was no longer regarded as a state of innocence after baptism. Instead, it was thought that parents had to be vigilant and ready to beat any signs of sin out of their children and, with a high mortality rate, the children had to be purified in readiness of death. Part of this instruction involved the literature produced , as it was heavily moralizing in its religiosity. Thomas White, a Nonconformist preacher, advised children to 'read no Ballads and foolish Books, but a Bible, and the *Plain mans pathway to Heaven*, a very plain holy book for you; get the *Practice of Piety*; Mr Baxter's *Call to the Unconverted*; Allens' *Allarum to the Unconverted*; read the Histories of the Martyrs that dyed for Christ . . . Read also often treatises of Death, and Hell and Judgement, and of the Love and Passion of Christ' (Cunningham 2006: 68). A sea change occurred, then, from the bawdy folk tales, ballads and romances of the Middle Ages, as children were becoming ever-more controlled ideologically to suit the conditions of a changing society. Described as 'probably the most influential children's book ever written', James Janeway's *A Token for Children, being an Exact Account of the Conversion, Holy and Exemplary Lives, and Joyful Deaths, of several young Children* (1671–72), precisely underlines this Puritan ethos. It is perhaps hard for us to imagine, given its preoccupation with childhood death, that this was described in the early nineteenth century as 'the most entertaining book that can be'. However, given how likely death could be for children in the sixteenth and seventeenth centuries, and the Puritans' obsession with ridding children of sin in order to possess God's grace, then such literature becomes more understandable. Janeway was directly influence by the theme of death in his writing, given his first-hand experience during the last Great Plague year in London, 1665, where he carried out pastoral work in the community. Children living in London, with all of its urban problems, were particularly vulnerable to infectious diseases. Childhood death is evident in Janeway's *A Token for Children*, with its emphasis on being prepared for death.

While these books might seem off-putting to the modern child, nevertheless they were extremely popular with children of that time; after all, the characters were the same ages as the readers, who felt an affinity with their fictional counterparts. Often, too, such dying stories portrayed children as being able to teach their parents to be more confident that they are going to heaven, so there was a degree of empowerment for the child reader. John Bunyan's *A Book for Boys and Girls* and *The Pilgrim's Progress* (1678) provide further examples of such popular moralizing tales.

During the Reformation period of the sixteenth and seventeenth centuries, Aesop's *Fables* was commonly used in schools, with various versions circulating, such as Robert Henryson's *The Morall Fabillis of Esope in Scottis Meter* (1570), John Ogilby's *The Fables of Aesop* (1651), Jean de La Fontaine's *Fables Choisies* (1668–93), and Sir Roger L'Estrange's *Aesop's Fables* (1692). Notably, John Locke's *Some Thoughts Concerning Education* (1693) recommended only two books as being suitable for children's education, namely *Reynard the Fox* and *Aesop's Fables*. While some challenged fables as being lies, given their fictional status, and, thus, prone to leading children toward deceitfulness, nevertheless Locke's recommendation meant that they remained popular into the eighteenth century and further, with rewritten versions appearing each few years, such as William Godwin's *Fables Ancient and Modern* (1805) and, even more recently, Vivian French and Korky Paul's *Aesop's Funky Fables* (1997).

In France, the literary or written fairy tale was gaining in popularity. The fairy tale is one type of appropriated oral tale (the wonder folk tale or magic tale). By the mid-seventeenth century, literary salons were established by aristocratic women who organized parlour games that included the use of folk motifs and narrative conventions. Those women who participated in the salon parlour games had to demonstrate their eloquent wit by spinning wondrous tales and from this emerged the term *conte de fees*, or fairy tale. So even in seventeenth-century French society, the literary fairy tale was produced for adults, arising from a desire by aristocratic women to offer alternative worlds to the society and roles defined for them by men. As such, these tales became an imaginary space in which women sought improved lives, and the tales were told in very collective and social ways, given that they were told in literary salons. Female characters were often given active and heroic roles, thus contradicting the static confinement of aristocratic women in the court of Louis XIV. While benefitting from the luxuries of court life, nevertheless these women were subject to the laws of a patriarchal society, in which they had little autonomy but, instead, were the property of men. Authors like Mademoiselle Bernard and Madame d'Aulnoy began to incorporate fairy tales into their fictional books, eventually publishing entire fairy tale collections. Publication of fairy tales in France was rapid between 1696 and 1704, with several writers producing versions, including Madame d'Aulnoy, Mademoiselle L'Heritier, Charles Perrault, Madame de la Force, Madame de Murat and Mademoiselle Bernard. The most famous version to appear would be Charles Perrault's *Histoires ou contes du temps passé* (1697). The parlour performance of such tales was for the amusement of the listeners, but also served to establish conventions about manners and *civilite* in French society. This meant that the content of the oral tales heard from servants or governesses were significantly altered to suit aristocratic ideologies. While it is generally believed that such written tales as Perrault's were intended for children, there is no evidence of this, although such adult texts did shape the fairy tales specifically developed for children. The tales were often translated, simplified and shortened, and spread across central Europe and Britain to the middle and lower classes, distributed by peddlers in a series of chapbooks. So, slowly these tales became adapted to include morals for children that reinforced a patriarchal society which was detrimental for women, even though women had, ironically, been originally responsible for writing the tales. It is no accident that male writers of fairy tales, including Perrault, were the ones who dominated the market. Fairy tales also served to uphold social class divisions, as they were intended for children of the upper classes, except for those available in chapbooks. Producing fairy tales in literary written form affected dissemination: oral tales had been told across class and age barriers, but the emerging print culture excluded the majority of children who could not read and who were, consequently, dependent upon an oral tradition of tale-telling. By writing tales down, also, they become more prone to being adapted to suit the time in which they are being written , and thus more influenced by the ideological demands of the day (Zipes 1991, 1994, Warner 1994, Seifert 1996, www.endicott-studio.com/rdrm/forconte.html).

A LITERATURE OF THEIR OWN?

Perrault's tales had been translated into English in 1729 and, along with other French tales, had been disseminated in chapbooks. Remember that by the seventeenth-century, Britain had undergone a Reformation, so many Protestant Puritans often opposed fairy tales. Generally, they were suspicious of the magic elements, or the way in which their fanciful content might encourage children to tell lies, and thus be considered ungodly. Of course, France was despised at this time as a Catholic country – in many ways the cultural Other of Britain – so one of the dominating reasons to fear fairy tales would, of course, have been based on religious differences. Despite this opposition, it became increasingly acceptable to include fairy tales in collections intended specifically for children, including Sarah Fielding's *The Governess; or, Little Female Academy* (1749) and Madame Leprince de Beaumont's *Magasin des enfants* (translated as *The Young Misses' Magazine*, 1757). Just as feminist critics like Elaine Showalter (1982) argue that women began to produce a literature that represented their own needs to offset the constraints of patriarchy, it could be argued that children were identified culturally as requiring their own particular books, though, of course, they were written and produced by adults and subject to the pedagogical and ideological needs of a patriarchal society. So, even though fairy tales were feared in some quarters, it is important to recognize that such stories were heavily didactic and included teaching girls morals and manners, particularly regarding gender roles, in the likes of 'Beauty and the Beast', where Beauty learns essential feminine qualities like self-sacrifice and self-effacement. Written to support the ideologies of the Court of Louis XIV, French literary fairy tales reflected and perpetuated patriarchal society's gender inequalities and maintained the status quo of social class hierarchies. Many children had been exposed to the fairy tale genre through chapbooks, while the introduction of the literary fairy tale ensured that several generations of aristocratic and bourgeois children were familiar with them by the end of the eighteenth century.

The features of fairy tales tended to include characters who were fairly two-dimensional, simple and flat, and who remain stable insofar as they don't really develop. There are usually strong contrasts or binary oppositions, such as between rich and poor, court life and country life, cottage and castle, good and evil. There is often, too, a sense of transformation or metamorphosis that occurs, be it in the form of a frog or a beast turning into a handsome prince, or a scullery maid into a beautiful princess. But, remember, that those who have been concealed by some kind of witchery are usually only ever restored to their proper former selves. In that sense the inheritors of riches from rags tend to be those who are royal or rich but under some curse. The status quo, then, is usually maintained.

With regards to the 'origins' of the fairy tale specifically written for children, then, it is almost impossible to give an exact date, but, given the way in which the genre of the fairy tale shifted itself towards upholding patriarchal society, it would be fair to assume that the fairy tale for children arose somewhere around the 1720s and 1730s. So the theme of female self-denial, such as is portrayed in, for example, 'Beauty and the Beast' or 'Cinderella' or 'Little Red Riding Hood', where the woman submissively consents to male authority, had very little in common with the female autonomy that aristocratic women had sought in the seventeenth-century French literary salons (Warner 1994, Haase [ed.] 2004, Hannon 1998). The change in fairy tale format, then, equates entirely with its changing social function for gender divisions, and its transformation into an institution for children. So, writers began to introduce more didactic stories, with a strong moralizing message for children. And boys and girls were often treated differently, where gender roles became more rigidly enforced, often with a view to instil so-called good sense and good manners and submissiveness in girls (Zipes 1991, Tatar 1999).

Despite the Enlightenment in the eighteenth century, there was an Evangelical revival at the end of the eighteenth century with the likes of the Religious Tract Society (RTS) being founded in 1799 intending to disseminate cheap religious stories in the nineteenth century, some of which were targeted at children and, notably, poor children. Beyond this, there were other evangelical and moralistic books produced, including Mary Martha Sherwood's *The History of the Fairchild Family* (1818, with other volumes in 1842 and 1847) and Maria Edgeworth's tales. So this uneasy tension between puritanical tales and chapbooks full of fanciful fables continued into the nineteenth century but there was an increasing appetite for works of fantasy and fairy tales, including the publication in 1823 in Britain of the Brothers Grimm's version of literary fairy tales and Hans Christian Andersen's fairy tales entitled *Wonderful Stories for Children* (1846). This increasing reading of pleasurable and fanciful tales helped to fuel what is known as the first Golden Age in children's literature, which occurred in the Victorian period (lasting from around 1850 until the early twentieth century). This triggered a revival in the fairy tale genre which had been looked upon with suspicion. Lewis Carroll's *Alice's Adventures in Wonderland* (1865) and *Through the Looking-Glass and What Alice Found There* (1872) are two of the most prominent new Victorian fairy tales. Others included Edward Lear's *A Book of Nonsense* (1846), John Ruskin's *The King of the Golden River* (1851), William Makepeace Thackeray's *The Rose and the Ring* (1854), Charles Kingsley's *The Water-Babies* (1863), George MacDonald's *The Princess and the Goblin* (1872) and *The Princess and Curdie* (1882), L. Frank Baum's *The Wonderful Wizard of Oz* (1900) and J.M. Barrie's *Peter Pan* (1911), while the established adult writer Oscar Wilde turned his hand to writing fairy tales.

To reiterate, in the eighteenth century, fairy tales contributed to the civilizing process of children, in order to prepare them for their place in society in terms of such demarcations as gender and social class. Charles Perrault is one of the earliest of these morally didactic fairy tales and his versions of such tales as *Little Red Riding Hood* reflect such issues. Perrault, writing from around the 1690s, began a trend of male writers responsible for the dominant fairy tale form of civilizing and moralizing, which included the German Brothers Grimm and Hans Christian Anderson from Denmark in the nineteenth century.

John Newbery's *A Little Pretty Pocket-Book* (1744) provides something of a pivotal moment and is often regarded as the first modern children's book, as it established a print culture of books marketed specifically for child readers. As such, this is the beginning of children's literature insofar as a clear printing branch arises and there is an attempt to entertain as well as to instruct. What Newberry and his rivals, such as Thomas Boreman (who published *Gigantick Histories* [1740–43]), or Thomas and Mary Cooper (who published *A Child's New Play-Thing* [1742] and the first-known collection of nursery rhymes, *Tom Thumb's Song Book* [1744]) achieved was the collection and distribution of such anonymous stories into books that started an industry of children's literature. While continuing to be didactic and moralizing, such books also attempted to amuse and entertain with the inclusion of rhymes, pictures, jokes, riddles and stories. At the turn of the century, the translation of Francois Fenelon's *Les Avantures de Telemaque fils d'Ulysse* (*The Adventures of Telemachus, Son of Ulysses*) (1699) offered a combination of adventure and moralizing, while Isaac Watt's *Divine Songs* (1715) was a collection of religious poetry that nevertheless contained playful verse.

Amid growing popularity, by the end of the century there were publishers who specialized in children's literature and specialist bookshops, as well. With the expansion of circulating libraries, children's books appeared and children's books were being reviewed in established literary journals. In 1802, Sarah Trimmer launched a specialized journal, the *Guardian of Education*. Several adults realized that it was possible to earn a decent living writing for children, including Sarah Trimmer and Richard Johnson, while several respected adult authors also turned their talents to children's books. For instance, Sarah Fielding wrote *The Governess* (1749) and Charlotte Smith admitted turning to children's books because she hoped it paid well and might be easier. Similarly, William Godwin acknowledged writing and publishing children's books as a move 'to establish a more secure income'. But, due to the expense of children's books, those from the poorer classes did not benefit from such expansion. While there were chapbooks readily available for a penny, nevertheless many of the poor were illiterate, and many continued to read books familiar to previous generations such as fables, romances, Bibles and chapbooks. Part of the reason for the availability of the new books, though, was a steadily improving economic, social and cultural climate: for instance, child mortality was decreasing, allowing parents to invest more fully in their children, both financially and emotionally. Such shifts were reflected in the books themselves: Newbery's story of *Goody Two-Shoes* charts a girl's rags to riches journey.

In the latter half of the century, while often secular, moral and instructive tales remained popular, such as Fielding's *The Governess*, Anna Laetitia Barbauld's *Lessons for Children* (1778), Thomas Day's *Sandford and Merton* (1783–89), Sarah Trimmer's *Fabulous Histories* (1786), John Aikin's *Evenings at Home* (1792–96), and Maria Edgeworth's stories beginning with *The Parent's Assistant* (1796) and continuing with the likes of *Early Lessons* (1801). Such tales tended to cast children as the main characters and included behavioural and moral lessons. While there were some stories with fantasy elements, for the most part these were realist texts that tended to have the purpose of reflecting and influencing the ordinary child reader's life. The other reason was the fear of encouraging children to tell lies as well as not firing up their imaginations with potentially "dangerous" associations. Isaac Watts warned,

Let not Nurses or Servants be suffered to fill their Minds with *silly Tales and with senseless Rhimes* . . . Let not any Persons that are near them terrify their tender Minds with dismal *Stories of Witches and Ghosts, of Devils and evil Spirits, of Fairies and Bugbears in the Dark*. This hath had a most mischievous Effect on some Children. (Cunningham 2006: 126)

Children's books, then, become an immensely powerful ideological tool in the surveillance and guidance of children and their parents in teaching children to be compliant, obedient and subservient. On the other hand, such tales offered children heroes and heroines that they could identify with and a literature which was separate from adult novels and directed specifically at their entertainment. As well as the continued seventeenth century split between Puritanism and chapbooks, there was the developing secular split of social class, as wealthy children were being steered away from the feared polluting influence of chapbooks.

REACHING THE FIRST GOLDEN AGE

With the coming of the Golden Age, as well as fantasy stories there was an increase in adventure tales, such as Frederick Marryat's *Children of the New Forest* (1847), R.M. Ballantyne's *The Coral Island* (1858) and Robert Louis Stevenson's *Treasure Island* (1883). School stories also became popular, including Harriet Martineau's *The Crofton Boys* (1841), Thomas Hughes's *Tom Brown's Schooldays* (1857) and F.W. Farrar's *Eric, or Little by Little* (1858), while realist domestic tales that combined imaginative elements also became popular, like Frances Hodgson Burnett's *Little Lord Fauntleroy* (1886) and *The Secret Garden* (1911), and Louisa May Alcott's *Little Women* (1868), *Good Wives* (1869) and *Little Men* (1871). Rather than being the subject of adult instruction, these tales tended to be more child-centred, insofar as the child is the protagonist and often teach adults, as the Victorians built heavily on the Romantic concept of childhood innocence and nature, evident in the likes of Kenneth Grahame's *The Golden Age* (1895) and *The Wind in the Willows* (1908). This shift in the significance of childhood in the British cultural psyche was also evident in the adult novels being produced which often depicted portrayals of childhood, including Charlotte Bronte's *Jane Eyre*, Emily Bronte's *Wuthering Heights*, Charles Dickens's *Oliver Twist*

(1839), *Bleak House* (1853), *Hard Times* (1854) and *Little Dorrit* (1855).

As the nineteenth century progressed, then, literature became geared more towards not instructing the child but, rather, centring the child itself as a point of innocence, where often the adult can return to a kind of Edenic space. So, in Frances Hodgson Burnett's *The Secret Garden*, for example, we see the adult character, Archibald Craven, being led significantly into the garden by the children. During times of social and political uncertainty and rapid change, childhood became ever more heavily invested as a site of innocent salvation by adult culture. As Adam Bresnick argues, 'for the past two centuries, the child has been the vehicle of our psychic transport to somewhere similar to Eden' (July 1998: 9). In that sense, with a gradual decline in religion childhood became a new space to worship. So the relationship between childhood, nature and the imagination begins to form a very close union. The impact of childhood innocence coincides with the centrality of the nuclear family as a buffer against an increasingly industrialized and hence, perceived to be, increasingly soulless or unimaginative society (think of, e.g., Charles Dickens's scathing criticism of the Industrial Revolution in his novel *Hard Times*, where a focus upon the learning of "facts" proves to be detrimental to the development of the imagination). Even children of the working classes, then, were gradually removed from the visibility of the workplace through a series of Parliamentary Acts, and placed into their "natural" environment of the home with mother, and the school. According to Hugh Cunningham, '[I]f adults were burdened with responsibilities, children should be carefree. If adults worked, children should not work [. . .] children were entitled to contact with nature' (Cunningham 1996: 160).

Of course, more cynically, one might argue that moving the lower-class child from the factory or the mine and into the realm of innocent childhood shared by its more affluent counterparts was, in fact, a way of preventing political unrest, the type that could lead to the bloody revolution still reverberating from France. Instances like the Swing Riots in the 1820s or the famous Massacre at Peterloo in 1819 all led the British Government of the day to be very alert to lower-class radical movements and the threat that they might pose to the British establishment. Arguably, the lower-class child, unlike the cherub-like privileged child, had to be instilled with innocence or, if you like, their childhood identity had to be created through discourse. Thus,

> While Wordsworth was extremely vocal in his support of fairy tales, he was careful to recommend religious tracts for the children of the poor. The increase in literacy amongst the poor was seen most often as a threat by those who had experienced the uprising of the labouring classes in France, as well as smaller rebellions on English soil [. . .] Whilst the child of nature, the familiar child of whom Wordsworth writes in *The Prelude*, reflects the Romantic image of the angel, the unblessed child must be controlled and kept from undermining the child whose natural place is "as father to the man". (Thacker and Webb 2002: 18)

One of these revolutionary fears came in the shape of Penny Dreadfuls, which were very popular with poor children. They were cheap (as their name implies) stories full of Gothic terror and page-turning sensationalism, condemned as corrupters of the moral fibre of Britain. Increasingly, religious tracts were produced to counter the popularity of such Penny Dreadful chapbooks and steer the impressionable lower-class child into less revolutionary pursuits. Having been taught to read with the 1870 Education Act, the poorer classes were now being encouraged to read the right books, as opposed to "literature of the streets" – that is those that would not pose any political or social unrest. So, clearly children's literature had become, by this stage, a hotly debated political and social topic, and the desire to socialize children or imbue them with an innocence is very much part of that agenda, while simultaneously claiming that childhood is somehow innately innocent. There is an inherent contradiction in this claim. As James R. Kincaid says, 'innocence is a faculty needed not at all by the child but very badly by the adult who put it there in the first place' (Kincaid 1992: 74). He goes on to say that 'the "child" is nothing more than what it is considered to be, nothing in itself at all' (Kincaid 1992: 90). According to this theoretical position, childhood is very much something of a creation. However, it would be a mistake to assume that children's literature merely reflected such social ideologies in a pedagogical manner; rather, it often negotiated with them and offered subversive alternatives. An example of this would be how Ballantyne's *The Coral Island* might be regarded as a heavily moralizing book but, on closer inspection, can reveal several ironic uncertainties relating to colonialism, Christianity and childhood innocence.

MATURING – THE SECOND GOLDEN AGE

The period around the First World War proved something of a dearth in children's literature, with school stories and war stories seeming to reflect on Britain's heroic heyday. Other books, like A.A. Milne's *Pooh* books (1926, 1928) and Hugh Lofting's *Dr Dolittle* series (1920–52) seemed to take refuge in pastoral retreats, while Arthur Ransome's *Swallows and Amazons* (1930) portrayed the security of family rural life. J.R.R. Tolkien's fantasy *The Hobbit* (1937) also offered a pastoral landscape, where the hero goes *There and Back Again* to the familiarity of home. This pastoral scene of nostalgic domesticity was also integral to Enid Blyton's works, including her series *The Famous Five* (1942–62) and *The Secret Seven* (1949–63). Even so, there are many hints of insecurity and threats forever impinging on the safety of home, while Britain viewed a Europe of rising Fascism and teetered on the uncertain brink of the Second World War.

By the 1960s, a new subsection of children's literature had emerged: teenage or young adult fiction, and with it came a fresh array of authors. There was a definite taste for fantasy, with the likes of C.S. Lewis's *Narnia Chronicles* (1950–56), Mary Norton's *The Borrowers* series (1952–82), William Golding's *Lord of the Flies* (1954), J.R.R. Tolkien's three-volume sequel to *The Hobbit*, *The Lord of the Rings* (1954–55), Philippa Pearce's *Tom's Midnight Garden* (1958), Susan Cooper's *The Dark Is Rising* volumes (1965–77), Patricia Wrightson's *The Ice Is Coming* series (1977–81), Alan Garner's novels, such as *Elidor* (1965) and *Red Shift* (1973), Richard Adams's *Watership Down* (1972), Ursula Le Guin's *Earthsea Chronicles* (1968, and first published in Britain from 1971), and, of course, Roald Dahl's collection. Other writers of this period include Raymond Briggs, while the likes of Louise Fitzhugh's *Harriet the Spy* (1964), Judy Blume's *Forever* (1975) and Jan Mark's *Thunder and Lightnings* (1976) demonstrate a taste for neo-realism. What is evident in such works is a tension between the adult world of conservatism, with its pastoral tropes and the child's world of modernity, corruption and danger. The children in these books are the ones attempting to find ways to negotiate with modern society and its rapid changes, and there are the beginnings of dealing with sexuality, such as Blume's *Forever* or Isabelle Holland's *The Man Without a Face* (1972), which tentatively explores homosexuality. Parents have become less reliable in these novels, with more open-ended, less neatly tied up closures, such as in the more subversive works of Le Guin or Garner. There is, however, still a sense of rural nostalgia in them but with a simultaneous feeling of a world ever changing and uncertain.

FACING THE FUTURE – THE THIRD GOLDEN AGE

By the late twentieth century, then, children's literature shows an array of unstable families and adults: the father figure is a far cry from the God-like omniscient figure of the Puritan days. Instead, it is the child who must navigate its own way through the dangers that unfold, including good versus evil, and the anxieties of growing up. This is not a world where children can remain forever young, as with *Peter Pan* but, instead, they must cope with the hostilities of life and are often left with unresolved endings, such as Mildred D. Taylor's *Roll of Thunder, Hear My Cry* (1976), Gillian Cross's *Wolf* (1990) or Melvin Burgess's *Junk* (1996). While these novels often carry the weight of the world on their young protagonist's shoulders, nevertheless there is still a desire for the maintaining of childhood innocence so strongly instilled from the Romantics. That goes hand in hand with attempts to continue to offer reassuring endings, even if they are not completely resolved. Often the pattern, then, follows the portrayal of home with its familiarity but perhaps dissatisfaction, then the dangers of the journey outwards to all that is uncertain and a circular return to a perhaps more secure place in the home.

As the twentieth century closed and the new millennium emerged, it is evident that the appetite for children's literature is stronger than ever and adults are increasingly turning to the category known as crossover fiction – that is that which appeals to both child and adult reader. Such prolific publishing has led critics to ponder whether we are now in a new golden age of children's fiction. With the huge popularity of books like J.K. Rowling's *Harry Potter* series (1997– 2007) and Philip Pullman's *His Dark Materials* trilogy (1995–2000) a massively influential cinematic output has come to complement these novels. But while there is a mass production of children's books, now, perhaps lamentably, the demands of

powerful publishers are narrowing the field towards a more for-
mulaic market. With such stringent influences driving the creative
output, does this mean that we are in the heyday of children's literature in its coming of age or, rather, is there a flood of what Peter
Hunt refers to as 'neo-conservative' (Maybin and Watson 2009: 81)
productions that all offer pretty much the same outlook. By that
he means a potential return to the didactic moralizing of books
reflecting and supporting the dominant social ideologies of contemporary society. This return to a reactionary era of ideologically
manipulated didactic texts driven by profit-orientated publishers
intent on playing it safe is certainly a phenomenon that troubles
Hunt (Maybin and Watson 2009: 81–2). However, subversive works
like Pullman's offer a significant challenge to this neo-conservative
argument. Equally, established writers of adult literature, like
Jackie Kay and Jeanette Winterson, are now foraging in the field
of children's fiction. With the influence of literary theory on many
of these writers, it is clear that their work is intertextual (exploring the links between its own narrative existence within a literary
continuum of previous texts), alluding not only to other children's
books but to adult fiction too. So, for instance, Pullman revisits the
biblical Book of Genesis, Milton's *Paradise Lost* and the poetry of
William Blake.

Contemporary fiction still utilizes familiar patterns, such as the
quest or journey motif and the shift from the familiarity of home
to the insecurity of beyond, but there is an altogether more mature
outlook. The taste for fantasy certainly continues, though there
are neo-realist texts, too, often dealing with the fragmentations
of modern urban family life. Given that Pullman and Rowling's
aforementioned books are series, then there is a tendency towards
open-endedness – so, for instance in Pullman's *Northern Lights*
(1995), it concludes with Lyra journeying towards a new world and
leaving her home behind. Rowling's series finally culminates in a
death and rebirth scene, with Harry's nemesis Voldemort finally
being overcome, but there is a sense that social divisions and prejudice are always present and, consequently, citizens must be watch-
ful. Other significant series include Michelle Paver's *Chronicles of
Ancient Darkness* (2004–09) which, although set in the Stone Age
and so equating childhood with something primitive and lost, is
nevertheless addressing urgent contemporary themes like environ-
mentalism. A gender revision of the adventure story is addressed in

Celia Rees's *Pirates* (2003), while Malorie Blackman's *Noughts and Crosses* (2001–06) trilogy engages with bleak contemporary issues like gang culture and racism. In terms of the urgency of climate change, Julie Bertagna's futuristic trilogy *Exodus* (2002), *Zenith* (2007) and *Aurora* (not yet published) charts the journey of Mara, an ordinary Scottish girl, to heroic saviour of her people. Stephenie Meyer's *Twilight* saga (2005–), on the other hand, draws on the tradition of Gothic vampire stories, but updated for a teenage readership, continuing in the vein of *Buffy the Vampire Slayer*. Other notable writers include Theresa Breslin, Gillian Cross, Michael Morpurgo, Jacqueline Wilson, Tom Pow, Keith Gray, Benjamin Zephaniah and Meg Rosoff.

There is a continuance of associations between childhood and healing of the family, social groups, and the environment that stems back to Romantic notions of childhood innocence but, on the other hand, there are greater challenges and uncertainties facing the child protagonists that cannot be easily resolved with happy endings. Accompanying the difficulties of pinning down children's literature has been its academic birth from Cinderella marginality to a growing rapidity at undergraduate and postgraduate levels of study. Beyond its cosmic rise with the help of literary theory has been the tussle over academic homes in terms of whether it should belong in education, given its concern with pedagogy, or English literary studies, given its textual materiality.

REVIEW

The term *children's literature* is complex and fluid in terms of intended readership and literary history, raising questions about:

Childhood's evolving state
Social class
Literacy
Gender
Different genres
Power and authority
Religion
Pleasure
Nationhood and Empire
Industrialization and urbanization

Mortality rates and improving social welfare conditions
Academic debate

READING

To gain a fuller understanding of the history and development of childhood read Hugh Cunningham, *Children and Childhood in Western Society Since 1500* (1995) and *The Invention of Childhood* (2006); Neil Postman, *The Disappearance of Childhood* (1982); Colin Heywood, *A History of Childhood: Children and Childhood in the West From Medieval to Modern Times* (2001).

For an introduction to children's literature read Peter Hunt, *An Introduction to Children's Literature (1994), Children's Literature: An Illustrated Histor*y (1995) and *Children's Literature* (2001); Kim Reynolds, *Children's Literature in the 1890s and the 1990s* (1994); M.O. Grenby, *Children's Literature* (2008); Janet Maybin and Nicola J. Watson (eds), *Children's Literature: Approaches and Territories* (2009); David Rudd, *The Routledge Companion to Children's Literature* (2010).

For some theoretical approaches to children's literature, consult Jacqueline Rose, *The Case of Peter Pan; Or the Impossibility of Children's Fiction* (1992); Fiona McCulloch, *The Fictional Role of Childhood in Victorian and Early Twentieth-Century Children's Literature* (2004); Peter Hunt (ed.), *Understanding Children's Literature* (2005); Kim Reynolds, *Modern Children's Literature: An Introduction* (2005).

RESEARCH

To what extent can children's literature be regarded as a problematic area? Give some specific examples of how this manifests itself.

In what ways has children's literature evolved from its beginnings to contemporary texts?

How far does children's literature correspond to social constructions of childhood?

Consider the debate between realism and fantasy in children's literature and how this has developed.

Choose two issues from the following and discuss their impact upon children's literature: print culture, literacy, social class, gender, religion, nation.

PART 2

TEXTS

CHAPTER THREE

TEXTS

LEWIS CARROLL – *ALICE'S ADVENTURES IN WONDERLAND* (1865) AND *THROUGH THE LOOKING-GLASS AND WHAT ALICE FOUND THERE* (1872)

Alice's Adventures in Wonderland was first published in 1865, at the height of what is referred to as the first Golden Age of children's literature. It was the first children's book to be regarded critically to be 'virtually entirely on the child's side' (Hunt 1994: 60). What this means is it is seen as moving away from the overtly didactic moralizing of earlier texts and toward an altogether more entertaining and pleasurable read, where the child is the central focus rather than being subject to adult authority.

The form of writing used by Carroll is known as nonsense, an area of literature with which he and his predecessor Edward Lear are commonly associated. Nonsense is considered to be anarchic in its outlook, often combining elements of both violence and death, all of which can be detected throughout both of the *Alice* books. Ultimately, reality itself is challenged through 'fantasy, nonsense, and parody' in ways that often push 'language and meaning toward dangerous limits of dissolution' (Shires 1988: 267). Playing with 'sense-making' combines both pleasure and terror because 'anarchy is both joyous and disturbing' (Shires 1988: 267–8). Victorian morality is subverted through the use of parody – well-known pious rhymes and verses are inverted, such as Isaac Watt's 'How doth the busy bee' which becomes 'How doth the little crocodile'. It is a morality that is regarded by Carroll's nonsense as hypocritical, where 'the child exposes the corruption of the world', for 'Alice is the disrupter of the Edenic myth of Victorian morality' (Natov 2006 [2003]: 50). The narrative flow is interrupted by songs, poems and even the illustrations of John Tenniel, a well-known political cartoon satirist in his day. As nonsense texts, the *Alice* books also invert the notion of childhood and its concomitant prelapsarian (an innocent state before the fall of adult experience) Eden, so that we are presented with 'a satiric antipastoral vision' (Natov 2006 [2003]: 51). The quest romance is parodied – the garden that Alice so desperately wants to enter is artificial and scary, even intimidating, so that '[t]he quest structures of the *Alices* offer graphic representations of a failed search for the warm joy and security of love' (Rackin (1987) in Bloom: 112). Although Alice strives to enter the 'loveliest garden you ever saw' (30), in keeping with pastoral associations of childhood and Eden, 'the Queen of Hearts' Croquet Grounds turn out to be the grounds for perfect (albeit laughable) hate and fury' (Rackin 1987: 112). The garden in *Wonderland*, far from a pastoral idyll, is actually a 'dreadfully confused and threatening version of the paradise the child in us seeks in its joys and desires' (Rackin 1987: 112).

Alice's Adventures in Wonderland and *Through the Looking-Glass* expose the instability of the self and its threatened annihilation. The prefatory poem in *Wonderland* reminds us that Alice is only a 'dream-child'. This directly confronts the Victorian preoccupation with sentimentalizing childhood innocence: discourses that purport to 'know' the child are subject to slippage and deferral as Alice's sense of self perpetually slides in a chaotic world where nothing makes sense to her, and childhood itself is merely the stuff of fantasy or dreams. Because nothing makes any sense, she constantly chases about in a bid to find meaning, but it continually collapses – she says in *Looking-Glass* that 'Somehow it seems to fill my head with ideas – only I don't exactly know what they are!' (197), and in *Wonderland* she says that the words she is confronted with 'seemed to her to have no sort of meaning in it, and yet it was certainly English' (97). It is a nonsense world – everything that is familiar to Alice as a child trying to make sense of her world is inverted, so that what she thought she knew turns out to be the opposite in this Wonder-Land of absurd logic (as a mathematician, Carroll was, of course, very interested in logic). While written for the pleasure rather than didactic instruction of the child, *Alice* is 'darkly comic, ironic, and distanced'

(Natov 2006 [2003]: 50) and Alice's search for certainty slips from her grasp since, 'All is in flux, no connection sure and solid' (Natov 2006 [2003]: 52).

According to Carroll's fiction, the presumed-innocent child exists very precariously in what is really a façade of innocent language when, in effect, that language is prone to numerous slippages and instabilities. The argument, put forward by Jacqueline Rose in *The Case of Peter Pan*, that children's literature was expected to have a transparent language and a sense of closure is complicated in the *Alice* books. Although a child, Alice exists in an adult world, subject to parental control in her world and to the absurdity of Wonderland in her dream world, which 'reveals a fractured adult world of nonsensical rules and conventions' (Natov 2006 [2003]: 51). In *Wonderland*, she falls asleep from boredom as her sister reads an adult book, while in *Looking-Glass*, 'she flees the Victorian hothouse of parental rules and conventionality to the other side of the mirror' (McCulloch 2004: 33), for 'there'll be no one here to scold me away from the fire. Oh, what fun it'll be, when they see me through the glass in here, and can't get at me!' (185). *Wonderland* involves an episodic dream structure in which Alice falls asleep from boredom because her older sister is reading a book without pictures, unlike Alice's own adventures, written by Carroll, which abound with illustrations by the political satirist John Tenniel. To reach her own adventure, though, Alice metaphorically travels *through* her sister's grown-up book – she 'peeped into the book her sister was reading' (25) – and so she is framed by an adult text. Alice as a fictional character in a children's story is framed by an omniscient adult narrator – she is thus controlled and constrained within the parameters of adult creativity. The Victorians may regard childhood as prelapsarian, but Alice faces the complexities of postlapsarian (the adult fallen world of experience) culture. Instead of preserving dominant Victorian views of childhood purity, Carroll's texts undermine it. The books themselves are far from straightforward and in many ways pre-empt and anticipate modernism's self-conscious awareness of the self and of the language that we rely upon to define that selfhood insofar as 'we notice the authenticity of Carroll's Darwinian representation of eroding Victorian certainty' (Natov 2006 [2003]: 54). As the British Empire waned and Victorian security of the nation's global dominance faltered, Christian belief in the coherence of the individual within a God created universe was being challenged by scientific thinkers like Charles Darwin. In *Wonderland*, Alice terrifyingly questions, 'if I'm not the same [... ...] who in the world am I? Ah, *that's* the great puzzle' (37).

Wonderland forges a link between the instability of identity and the act of consumption: both meet in the text at the point where language proves to be at its most unreliable. Alice's size and shape constantly fluctuate and each time this is triggered by an oral act – linguistic signs, such as 'DRINK ME' or 'EAT ME' manoeuvre her into the position of market consumer of produce that she feels is aimed at her. The Marxist critic, Louis Althusser, refers to this as a process of ideological interpellation where the individual is inter-pellated (or hailed) to identify with a label and step into the con-structed position of socialized subject that awaits. Like advertising campaigns where the consumer feels that they are being personally addressed to identify with a product, Alice believes that consumer goods in Wonderland are for her. When Alice is confronted with a bottle marked 'DRINK ME', she assumes that it is safe, given that there is no mention of poison on the bottle. She demonstrates a naïve trust in language – just because it is not labelled poison, Alice assumes that it must be safe. As she falls down the rabbit hole, 'she took down a jar from one of the shelves [... ...] labelled 'ORANGE MARMALADE', but to her great disappointment it was empty' (27). Alice's frustration begins to alert her to the realization that linguistic signs (or words) are arbitrary – what is written on a bot-tle or a jar may not correlate to its contents. Just as the marmalade jar is empty when it signifies that it holds marmalade, so too is all language empty. In *Wonderland* childhood, too, is shown to be a label that is devoid of meaning beyond that which Western culture produces, for '[t]hat we trust language to define, identify, and con-nect us with the outside world places us in danger' (Natov 2006 [2003]: 52).

Sigmund Freud argued that childhood sexuality involved stages, such as the oral and anal stage of sexual development. The oral stage is a union forged with the mother's body at the pre-Oedipal stage of development, when the child receives all of its nourishment and pleasure from that relationship. In children's literature, time and again, that oral phase is dramatized through a plenitude of eating. In *Wonderland*, Alice is obsessed with an orality impulse. Even her cat, Dinah, *sounds* very much like diner and is a figure that threat-ens many of the creatures in Wonderland with annihilation, such as

TEXTS

the Mouse, a stock dinner for the feline diet. Although Dinah is a source of pleasure for Alice, Carroll suggests that her association of 'the word "cat" to denote comfort' nevertheless 'means danger to the Mouse' and, as such, 'we are limited by our own singular perceptions and experiences, and therefore doomed to a kind of absurd alienation' (Natov 2006 [2003]: 52). All of the time, though, Alice is trying to keep some kind of control, or order, on this chaotic oral aggression which drives the text but, in acts of Freudian slippage, it keeps pushing through to the surface – for example, Alice resolves not to talk about Dinah's success in hunting prey and then immediately lets slip that 'she'll eat a little bird as soon as look at it' (53). She is locked in a struggle of oral violence and, ultimately, the fear is that she herself will be swallowed up in a dark void by the very products that she is instructed to consume, worrying that 'it might end [. . .] in my going out altogether, like a candle' (32).

It can be helpful to think about *Through the Looking-Glass* in relation to the psychoanalytic arguments of Jacques Lacan in his essay 'The Mirror Stage'. Lacan revises Freud's work on the Oedipal conflict – at the resolution of this conflict, he says, we identify with society's Symbolic Order. That "reality" is made sense to us through language, which is when we acquire our sense of self, but it is a self that is really constructed through social discourses, as we become a social subject. Prior to this, the pre-Oedipal phase involves an inseparable union with the Mother, in which all of our desires and impulses are met in an existence that does not require utterance through language. It is at the separation of this pre-Oedipal stage (which Lacan calls the Imaginary) at the time of the Oedipal conflict that a separation occurs between child and Mother and this separation leads to a sense of lack. That lack signifies that our desires and needs will not be met by the Mother's union, but must now be vocalized ourselves within the Symbolic Order. The trouble is that what we desire or lack is the pre-Oedipal union that existed prior to language in the Imaginary, so our lack can never be addressed in the Symbolic Order. Instead, according to Lacan, we go through life trying to plug the hole in our soul with various people or objects that we think will heal that desire – desire, however, is never satisfied, and so we continue to seek. Notice that both of the *Alice* books convey a quest motif, where Alice questions and searches as she travels through the text, and what is perpetually at stake is her sense of self. Part of this Oedipal resolution, for

Lacan, involves what he calls the 'mirror stage'. If we imagine a small child contemplating itself in a mirror – Lacan's so-called 'mirror stage' – 'we can see how, from within this "imaginary" state of being, the child's first development of an ego, of an integrated self-image, begins to happen' (Eagleton 1993: 164). Although the child is still physically uncoordinated, its reflected image in the mirror is gratifyingly unified, for 'it has begun the process of constructing a centre of self' yet 'the child "misrecognizes" itself in it' (Eagleton 1993 [1983]: 164–5). That misrecognition and separation between self and reflected image will continue in a process of socialization in which the ego is formed, as being distinct and separate from what we are not; that is, that which is other to our self. What both *Wonderland* and, particularly with its use of the mirror, *Through the Looking-Glass* examines is the split that opens up between our conscious and unconscious – hence why Alice is often referred to as having schizophrenic traits.

Alice passes from the socially recognizable world of the Symbolic Order *through* the looking-glass to the other side, the dimension where what Lacan calls the Imaginary lurks in the depths of our unconsciousness, in a bid to reconnect with the unified self of the pre-Oedipal phase. Julia Kristeva calls Lacan's Imaginary the Semiotic. In this world beyond the familiar, beyond the taken-for-granted, the very essence of reality is questioned, as everything knowable in Alice's world is catapulted towards chaotic uncertainty. So in *Through the Looking-Glass*, 'one is immediately tempted to think of the Mirror Stage (in Jacques Lacan, *Writings*), and to take the whole adventure for a figurative representation of the imaginary construction of self, the ego, through reflexive identification' (Cixous 1982: 238). This is just one way of interpreting Carroll's nonsense texts and cannot be the decisive reading. But this notion of being on the other side of the looking-glass allows Carroll to play a game of 'let's pretend' (180), insofar as the accepted givens of society no longer hold sway and the multiple possibilities of the unconscious realm seep through. That becomes a powerful political metaphor for thinking beyond the constraints of so-called reality and a unified selfhood since her identity defies social stability and cohesion. Instead, she enters an uncanny world where her identity and her control of language are perpetually undermined.

To think of Freud and Lacan's concepts of the unconscious requires us to think about this relationship between the pre-Oedipal imaginary (or Kristeva's semiotic) and the post-Oedipal symbolic order. It is during this pre-Oedipal stage that the child is driven by oral compulsions and after the Oedipal conflict that they enter into (the patriarchal) structure of language, called by Lacan the symbolic order or the Law of the Father/phallus. In *Wonderland* and in *Looking-Glass*, a tension erupts between these two different modes of the imaginary or semiotic and the symbolic order. Alice as "dream-child" is placed in a dream realm of the unconscious which is a state driven by all of the pre-Oedipal desires repressed upon entering society's symbolic order. Contradicting or undermining that, however, is the desire for Alice to exist in a recognizable social world of the symbolic. *Wonderland*'s dreamscape forces us to rethink what we take for granted to be normal and to question its insanity or madness (a theme that pervades with the tea party and the Cheshire Cat). Meaning is not innate, but is something cultural that we learn, and the unconscious dimension of Carroll's text indicates that the division between reality and dream or normal and mad are very fine lines indeed. Alice as a 'dream-child' must constantly renegotiate the conditions of her reality. As such, she is as disembodied as the Cheshire Cat, madly fluctuating between arbitrary linguistic signs, only to concede that 'I'm never sure what I'm going to be, from one minute to another!' (77) simply 'because I'm not myself, you see' (67). The fictional character, Alice, then, resists a comfortable notion of coherent childhood innocence and demonstrates that we are all prone to the shifts of cultural conditioning.

Both *Alice* texts pre-empt the poststructuralist argument that there is no material substance behind language. Instead, there is only a chain of signifiers that are in a constant state of flux and deferral. Rene Descartes's notion that 'I think therefore I am', (I cannot doubt that I exist because by the very act of doubting that I exist, I am existing), is inverted by Carroll. Instead, he pre-empts deconstruction theories, such as Jacques Derrida's concept of Difference. Derrida alludes to the Western belief that meaning depends on what he calls 'a metaphysics of presence'. He is referring to our assumption or belief in an inherent meaning or truth underlying the contingency of existence. He calls this belief in unified meaning, which underpins Western conceptual thought, logocentricism. Derrida argues that meaning is constantly deferred, that it is unstable and subject to a perpetual play with other meanings (e.g., the concept good, as originating in God, only carries meaning by depending on its opposite of evil. So how could a notion of goodness have pre-existed Satan's original sin?). Likewise, according to Lacan, our identity has no authentic point of origin or unified self; it begins in a fantasy or mirror image. For Lacan, selfhood is merely a continual state of deferral enacted by the displacement of desire for the mother experienced in the pre-Oedipal stage. This is perpetuated by a sense of dislocation and lack caused at the Oedipal crisis. Therefore, Lacan replaces Descartes's concept of 'I think therefore I am' with 'I think I am where I am not'. Given that we, as social subjects, rely upon language to make sense of our world and, indeed, our selves, the implication is that we too are not constant, but rather prone to fluid mutation and multiplicity. In turn childhood, (dis)embodied in the figure of Alice, is demonstrated in Carroll's texts to be an insubstantial entity constructed through linguistic discourse.

An example of textual insecurity in *Wonderland* would be Alice's failed attempt to solve the unanswerable riddle posed by the Mad Hatter of 'Why is a raven like a writing-desk?' (95) or the interchangeable reference to whether cats eat bats or vice versa (28). Carroll himself insisted that the Mad Hatter's riddle had no answer, but it did not dissuade multiple attempts by readers to interpret it anyway, suggesting that adult culture continually strives to pin things down, to fix meaning, to close texts and acquire certainty – exactly as Alice tries to do. But the *Alice* books are not meant to be reduced to one interpretation; they are nonsense writing – they are fluid and multiple: they are 'exactly like a riddle with no answer', as Alice herself says. In that sense, to define is to restrict, just as childhood itself is restricted through definition. The narrative of both *Wonderland* and *Through the Looking-Glass* is disjointed and multiply layered rather than coherent and unified – for instance, the poems and John Tenniel's illustrations interrupt the flow of narrative linearity, rendering the text fluid and mobile. One of the ways that readers have attempted to reduce or simplify meaning in *Wonderland* and *Looking-Glass* is by attributing them to purely biographical readings of Carroll himself (which is somewhat futile because Carroll was a performed, constructed identity). The author instead tries to open up reader debate in his works, leaving them to the multiple possibilities that reader response may allow. His poem *The Hunting of the Snark* was another nonsense verse that people have desperately tried to pin down, while Carroll remarked, 'As to the meaning of the Snark [. . . . . .], I'm very much afraid I didn't mean anything but nonsense! Still, you know, words mean more than we mean to express when we use them; so a whole book ought to mean a great deal more than the writer means' (Collingwood 1898: 173). Although a Victorian writer, Carroll's approach to fiction can be regarded as proto-Modernist and pre-empting deconstructionism.

Carroll was interested in photography and he is known to have been particularly interested in photographing young girls. Much psycho–biographical interpretation exists, conjecturing whether that made him a paedophile or sexually repressed. The rise of photography in the Victorian period was a significant instance in terms of cultural theory because it captured images of the reflected self. Another type of lens arose at this time, too: looking-glasses or mirrors became widely available and more affordable in Victorian society as one could look at oneself and ponder how to improve one's appearance in a world of possibility that promoted hard work and thrift, where the onus was put upon the individual for their social failure or success (Samuel Smiles's *Self-Help* was published in 1859). If the mirror symbolizes the social gaze, then its reflection back at you meant that you had internalized that gaze and created a self that strove to improve upon the image. Charles Kingsley's novel *The Water-Babies* was published in 1863, just two years before *Wonderland* and he, too, draws attention to the importance of the mirror in constructing a social subject. When the poor chimney-sweep Tom mistakenly ends up in the bedroom of the rich young girl, whose house he has been hired to sweep, 'looking round, he suddenly saw, standing close to him, a little ugly, black, ragged figure [. . . . . .] He turned on it angrily. What did such a little black ape want in that sweet young lady's room? And behold, it was himself, reflected in a great mirror, the like of which Tom had never seen before' (Kingsley 1863: 17). Social Darwinism associated the lower classes with evolutionary degeneration.

In *Through the Looking Glass*, Alice as child subject passes through that social mirror to the Other side. In *Looking-Glass*, Alice is on a train and the Guard looks at her 'first through a tele-scope, then through a microscope, and then through an opera-glass' (218). Each reflected image positions Alice at a different size. As child, and specifically a female child, she is constantly subjected to the scrutiny of the constructive gaze. She is freeze-framed in her textual world of childhood, never to escape its covers and grow up, unlike Alice Liddell (the real child to whom the story was first told), who did grow up. The fictional child, then, becomes a metaphor for what adult culture desires of childhood – that it will remain a constant site of innocence, an anchor in an ever-changing world. In the prefatory poem to *Looking-Glass*, it says: 'I and thou/Are half a life asunder', where narrator and child have been divided by 'envious years' to which innocence is lost to the 'unwelcome bed' – with connotations of marriage bed and, ultimately, death bed. In essence, to reach adulthood is itself perceived as a form of death, with childhood passing away. *Looking-Glass* (1872), published seven years after *Wonderland*, is generally considered by critics to be a much bleaker story than its predecessor *Wonderland* and the opening setting of winter is read as a metaphor of this bleakness, sterility, age and loss. It also depicts the tension between the progression of the Industrial Revolution and a desire to return to a prelapsarian golden age only seen as attainable through childhood. For Natov, 'This antipastoral landscape belongs to industrialized England where its instrument, the train, is more important than the humans it transports' (Natov 2006 [2003]: 53). The train's dominance towers over the human, for the 'tickets are larger than Alice, and "the smoke alone is worth a thousand pounds a puff"' (Natov 2006 [2003]: 53).

On the other side of the looking-glass, a world which questions the reality of the Symbolic Order opens up. In this imaginary space, children are not shown to be sites of innocence, but instead are referred to as 'fabulous monsters'. This observation is made in the 'Lion and the Unicorn' chapter, where the Unicorn, itself a fantasy beast of mythical dimensions, ironically addresses Alice (the 'dream-child') with the claim that he thought children were 'fabulous monsters' (287) or unreal. Of course, Alice *is* a 'fabulous monster' in the sense that she is a fictional character, just like the Unicorn, both of them featuring in Carroll's text. But, the implication is that all children are fictional products created through adult discourses. Both childhood and unicorns share the same mythical dimensions, as identity is reduced to a game of masquerade, where the Unicorn says to Alice, 'if you'll believe in me, I'll believe in you' (287). Alice epitomizes childhood as 'a fictional character' who is 'controlled by adult authorship and, ultimately, insubstantial

[. . . . . .] children are recognized in Carroll's self-aware text to be nothing but "fabulous monsters", mythopoetic creatures of contemporaneous culture' (McCulloch 2004: 25–6).

The threat of insubstantiality, annihilation and nothingness that features in *Wonderland* continues through the story of *Looking-Glass*, where Alice must participate as a pawn in a game of chess, self-consciously observing the 'great huge game of chess that's being played – all over the world' (207–8). In Wonderland, the game motif pervades the text, particularly the concept of cards, whereas in *Looking-Glass*, chess is the puzzling game. It is a metaphor for concepts of power where the pawn is manoeuvred and manipulated. The pinnacle of Alice's anxiety that she may not be who she thinks she is occurs in the Tweedledum and Tweedledee chapter. Her desperate compulsion to cling on to a recognizable reality forged in the Symbolic Order of Victorian patriarchal society is shattered at this point when she is told, 'You know very well you're not real [. . . . . .] You won't make yourself a bit realer by crying' (239). She is forced to realize that 'you're only a sort of thing in his dream! If that there King was to wake [. . . . . .] you'd go out – bang! – just like a candle!' (238). Her hopes of a fixed reality and identity are lost amid insurmountable layers of textuality and identities as part of the Red King's dream, who is part of her dream, who is part of the narrator's story, who is part of a fictional text, whose author himself has adopted a pseudonym.

Looking-Glass's relationship with Romantic discourse is important, since childhood innocence is interlinked with nature, and children's literature often includes pastoral settings. Alice is consumed by a desire to reach, what she thinks is, a beautiful garden in *Wonderland*. But, when she finally does enter the garden, she finds that it is artificially constructed (the roses are being painted) and filled with violent death threats – hardly the ideal space that Rousseau had in mind. Echoing humanity's Fall and expulsion from Eden, Alice falls down a rabbit-hole and is referred to as a 'serpent' (75), associating her as a female child with Eve's temptation by the serpent in Eden. *Through the Looking-Glass* contains a scene with an Edenic childhood space. In 'the wood where things have no names', Alice wanders with the Fawn in a state of prelapsarian harmony: 'they walked on together through the wood, Alice with her arms clasped lovingly round the soft neck of the Fawn' (226–7). This is an Imaginary pre-Oedipal space – a wood where the Symbolic Order's language and labels have no meaning and where the child (emblematic in cultural discourses as an innocent saviour) can harmoniously coexist in ecological oneness with her surrounding environment. It is both a space of prelapsarian innocence and semiotic erotic wild Otherness (framed by a postlapsarian Symbolic Order on the side of the looking-glass that houses the conventional Victorian society from which Alice escaped). But, as anarchic nonsense, this is a parody of innocent childhood, where nothing is fixed or reliable. Alice is a pawn who is manoeuvred through the text by the invisible hand of a postlapsarian omniscient narrator. She does not remain in Edenic bliss with the Fawn, but instead faces the separation and lack from the Symbolic Order. On leaving the wood, 'the Fawn gave a sudden bound into the air, and shook itself free from Alice's arm' (227). Harmony is rent asunder as the cultural order imposes its system of classification, creating binaries of self and other so 'a sudden look of alarm came into its beautiful brown eyes, and in another moment it had darted away at full speed' upon the animal's realization that 'I'm a Fawn [. . . . . .] And dear me! you're a human child!' (227). Ironically, Alice, supposedly an innocent child, demonstrates its antithesis by embracing the cultural order separating her from nature, saying, 'I know my name now [. . . . . .] that's *some* comfort. Alice – Alice – I won't forget it again' (227). So 'Alice can enter that preoedipal Edenic state of boundarilessness, only to be severed from her connection with the fawn once language intervenes, and the things regain their borders' (Natov 2006 [2003]: 52).

Alice reminds us that childhood is not a site of timeless perpetual paradise, but, on the contrary, is very much part of the society which produces it. Alice depends, for her sense of self, upon the labels that Western culture produce around her. But these labels and the language that describes them are utterly empty of substance. As Humpty Dumpty says, 'When *I* use a word [. . . . . .] it means just what I choose it to mean – neither more nor less' (269). Typically, Alice feels the need to cling on to what her previous reality has taught her to be the case about meaning and about identity, so she responds with 'The question is [. . . . . .] whether you *can* make words mean so many different things' (269). That conversation echoes what Carroll himself suggested about trying to detect meaning in his texts. Reversing the social mirror, Carroll's text demands that we recognize how dependent we are upon discourses for our sense of self and our external reality, which we take for granted as normality. The world beyond the looking-glass inverts the norm and privileges the chaotic mass of the unconscious drives that lurk beneath the surface. The security of selfhood is shown to be extremely fragile, problematizing the cultural tendency to pre-serve childhood as an untainted sanctuary.

ROBERT LOUIS STEVENSON – *TREASURE ISLAND* (1883)

Piracy and the various forms that it takes in relation to both the production of Robert Louis Stevenson's *Treasure Island* and its fic-tional content, and a sense of doubleness that crops up repeatedly in various formats are vital. The most famous text by Stevenson that involves this duality is *The Strange Case of Dr Jekyll and Mr Hyde* in which Mr Hyde is the disfigured, concealed Other beneath Dr Jekyll's culturally acceptable façade. Mr Hyde literally hides within the identity of his alter ego, Dr Jekyll. When Stevenson was a young student at Edinburgh University, he frequented the seedier underbelly of Edinburgh's Old Town, including the bars and brothels. This was in direct contrast to his respectable middle-class family life in the New Town part of the city. Stevenson was fasci-nated with the city's respectable façade which conceals a darker Gothic undertone, which seemed to mirror his own tastes as a young man. It is no surprise that this doppelganger effect pervades his fic-tion, including *Treasure Island*, since '*The Strange Case of Dr Jekyll and Mr Hyde* [1886] has become the literary representation of the gulf between Victorian outward respectability and inward corrup-tion' (Gifford et al. 2002: 403). Though set in London, critics often argue that the text corresponds 'with Stevenson's home in polite Edinburgh, adjacent to slums and vice', arguing 'that the tale is another metaphor for Stevenson's questioning of outward virtue and social status' (Gifford et al. 2002: 403).

Treasure Island was first published in novel form in 1883 (it appeared in serial form in *Young Folks* magazine 1881–82), 25 years after Ballantyne's *The Coral Island* was published. Stevenson was an avid reader of Ballantyne's novel and he pays homage to 'Ballantyne the brave' in *Treasure Island*'s prefatory poem, 'To the Hesitating Purchaser'. He claims to be following a tradition of boy's adventure stories, known as Robinsonades (named after Daniel Defoe's *Robinson Crusoe*, 1719). From the outset, Stevenson is alerting us to the fact that he is borrowing from other texts and traditions in order to create his own piece of fiction. He wrote an account called 'My first book' about *Treasure Island*, where he readily admits that 'I believe plagiarism was rarely carried farther [. . . . . .] It may be, I care not a jot' (Stevenson 1985: 196). Stevenson is admitting to being a pirate in the sense that he is copying and revising earlier forms for his own ends. He targets this book towards the market of children's literature, writing in a letter to his friend W.E. Henley that 'there's more coin in it than in any amount of crawlers [. . . . . .] I'll make this boy's business pay' (Maixner 1981: 124–5). Like the fictional pirates of *Treasure Island*, the novel's author also hopes to make lucrative financial gains from the book (he even sounds like a pirate in the previous quotation). A sense of doubleness occurs between outer piracy and inner fictional piracy, as the form and the content of the book correspond to each other in the pursuit of bounty. Likewise, Stevenson played a double identity when the novel was first published in serial form, publishing it under the pseudonym of Captain George North, so blurring the divide between internal fiction and external reality.

Stevenson is alluding to the fictionality of all literary texts and, indeed, narratives that profess to be truthful. Just as *Treasure Island* is self-referential, with its multiple intertextual references and the author's own critical debate about it, Stevenson discusses the problem of 'Truth' in 'A Humble Remonstrance' (1884), arguing that 'on a more careful examination truth will seem a word of very debateable propriety, not only for the labours of the novelist, but for those of the historian' (Eigner and Worth 1985: 216). Like Carroll, Stevenson tends to pre-empt poststructuralist thinking for, according to Roland Barthes in his essay 'The Death of the Author', all literary texts are as pirated as Stevenson's claims to be. Barthes writes,

> a text is not a line of words releasing a single "theological" meaning (the "message" of the Author-God) but a multi-dimensional space in which a variety of writings, none of them original, blend and clash. The text is a tissue of quotations drawn from the innumerable centres of culture [. . . . . .] the writer can only imitate a gesture that is always anterior, never original. (Barthes 1977: 146)

The desire for children's literature to exact a kind of innocent truth, then, is ultimately futile because narrative is always second-hand. As well as pointing out the fictionality of *Treasure Island*, Stevenson also clearly questions the truth of history, including Western history and the complex nature of representing the past through narrative. Like Ralph Rover in *The Coral Island*, in Stevenson's novel the narrator, Jim Hawkins, is also reconstructing and retelling an alleged boyhood adventure, from the hindsight of adulthood. In the text there is a duality or doubling of character because under the façade of the child lurks the experience of an adult narrative. At the outset of the novel there is a self-conscious awareness of the act of storytelling and the creation of a narrative that ultimately becomes the fictional text *Treasure Island*. Hawkins consciously 'takes up [his] pen' (1), thus performing the role of story-teller, taking us back to 'the year of grace 17–' in order to apparently merely provide a record of actual events, at the behest of 'Squire Trelawney' and 'Dr Livesey' (1883: 1). He tells us in the opening lines that he will 'write down the whole particulars about Treasure Island, from the beginning to the end, keeping nothing back but the bearings of the island' (1). By holding back the very location, of course, Hawkins signals that this will not be a transparent record of events, but will be a dislocated, fluidly unstable work of metafictional dimensions. He also frames the narrative here with a language steeped in adult references, such as the terminology of legal obligations.

Part of the textual self-conscious awareness of fictionality is this awareness of doubleness – there is a sense of a surface appearance that seeks to conceal that which lurks beneath an apparently innocent façade, with a hidden agenda. One of the most poignant deceptive performers in the text is the pirate Long John Silver (who has, interestingly, proved to outlive all of the other characters in this novel – most people, even if they have never read the book – will know of the infamous Long John Silver). Interestingly, he is 'roundly accused of playing double' (165) which is, we are informed, the 'exact thing that he was doing' (165). As a dual character, Silver disrupts the cultural construction of pirate as Other, as drunken, as uneducated, as white yet dark-skinned, etc. On the contrary, 'he was very tall and strong [. . . . . .] plain and pale, but intelligent [. . . . . .] I thought I knew what a buccaneer was like – a very different creature, according to me, from this clean and pleasant-tempered landlord' (42–3). Discourses which claim to know particular identities are overturned in the text, as Hawkins realizes that narratives cannot be trusted (just as we should not necessarily trust his narrative). Silver is not a drunken sailor nor is he uneducated – he 'had good schooling in his young days and can speak like a book when so minded' (54). To 'speak like a book' on the one hand involves a degree of educated intelligence and loquaciousness – on the other hand, it involves the use of language to deceive and conceal one's hidden agenda. In that sense, Silver is silver-tongued in his capacity to draw in and persuade his listener of his reliability. It is Silver's successful storytelling that draws Hawkins to him – he mistakenly narrates that 'Long John Silver told the story from first to last, with a great deal of spirit and the most perfect truth' (46). Hawkins is so trusting of Silver that he insists he 'would have gone to bail for the innocence of Long John Silver' (45). Ironically, underneath Silver's 'innocence' lies murderous deceit, just as underneath the proclaimed innocence of Jim Hawkins's narrative lies a postlapsarian adult agenda. Just as Silver lures and flatters Hawkins, so, too, does Hawkins's narrative draw in and deceive its reader.

In Ballantyne's novel, there is confusion between the forces of legitimate and illegitimate colonial power – in *Treasure Island* these boundaries become even less clearly defined. Whereas in *The Coral Island*, the savage Other is externally located in the South Pacific portrayal of cannibals, in Stevenson's later novel there are no savages, there are no inhabitants of Treasure Island. The only figure they do come across is the marooned pirate, Ben Gunn, another Western white man who sought the same treasure that both Silver's pirates and Hawkins's upstanding comrades hope to unearth. It is with deceptive irony that the respectable English claim the higher moral ground in *Treasure Island* because they, too, are shown to be playing a double role of deception. Squire Trelawny hypocritically proclaims, 'What were these villains after but money? What do they care for but money? For what would they risk their rascal carcases but money'. But in the same breath, he then says, 'If we have the clue you talk about, I fit out a ship in Bristol dock, and take you and Hawkins here along, and I'll have that treasure if I search a year [. . .] We'll have [. . .] money to eat' (33–4). A double-standard arises between pirates and respectable English gentlemen, each desperately charting a course to Treasure Island, a location whose very name smacks of the desire for absolute wealth. Stevenson's text, then, creates a tension between colonial enterprise and piracy, when both ultimately seek the same avaricious goal.

Thus, there is a doubling of what is meant by a 'gentleman of fortune' in the novel: on the one hand, a 'gentleman of fortune' refers to a self-made Victorian colonial trader, the proud figure of Empire but, on the other, it refers to 'a common pirate' (59). Historically, the links between pirates and colonizers were very permeable: an example would be 'Capt. Kidd's Anchorage' (64), which refers to William Kidd, a Scottish sailor who became a pirate (205). Silver takes this blurred boundary further by citing a desire to enter Parliament, the ultimate symbol of the British Establishment. When he casts off his costume of pirate, Silver hopes to enter the league of gentleman: he says 'Dooty is dooty [. . .] When I'm in Parlyment, and riding in my coach, I don't want none of these sea-lawyers in the cabin a-coming home, unlooked for, like the devil at prayers' (61). His corrupt enunciation of Parliament and duty suggests that there is a corruption at the heart of British society itself, while Hawkins's narrative takes the events of the novel back to the year '17–'. This eighteenth-century setting potentially draws on the corrupt political regime of Robert Walpole who was found guilty of corruption and dismissed from the House of Commons, only to be returned the following year, quickly moving into positions of political prominence. So Parliament itself 'plays double': beneath the façade of public representation lies a hotbed of power struggles and the desire for wealth. Interestingly, *Treasure Island*'s publication coincided with 'The passage of the Corrupt and Illegal Practices Act of 1883', which 'outlawed the use of paid agents and their customary usage of bribery, treating, assault, or abduction to ensure that electors turned up on polling days and that they voted the right way' (Caine 1997: 124).

Like Ballantyne, Stevenson was Scottish – this is another doubling, in the sense that the author of *Treasure Island* is a subject of the British Empire but is simultaneously capable of critiquing that Empire from the position of colonized subject. Alan Riach makes an interesting comparison between colonialism and childhood, arguing that 'A nation without statehood is the condition of childhood, and children, like Scots, are both the victims and the perpetrators of empire. Like Jim, they run toward imperial certainty even as they subvert it' (Riach 1996: 187). Since the Act of Union in 1707, Scottish writing and culture has said to be suffering from a kind of split personality, where Scots are estranged from their own nation, dispossessed from a culture and history that is subsumed into a wider Britain, always perceived as being the inferior of their Anglo neighbours (rectified in 1999 with Scottish Devolution and the establishment of the Holyrood parliament). That notion of duality in Stevenson's writing reflects this Caledonian schizophrenia and becomes part of 'a school of Scottish fiction which has its own particular and almost obsessive preoccupation with divided self and divided family within divided community and nation' (Gifford et al. 2002: 327). Another significant duality in terms of Stevenson is that he is a Victorian writer who bridges the approaching twentieth century. He adheres on one level to Victorian realism but, at the same time, his writing challenges realism as it is proto-Modernist (like *Alice*) and is a tale of romantic adventure. His work demonstrates modernist traits in its self-conscious awareness of its own status as fiction, and in the preoccupation with the unreliability of language, of narratives to reflect reality, when they are always in the business of shaping and constructing that reality. To pursue the modernist facets of Stevenson's work, read Alan Sandison's *Robert Louis Stevenson and the Appearance of Modernism*. The indication is that Jim Hawkins's narrative lens will be fraught with difficulties and contradictions, not with childhood simplicity.

Another doubling in the novel occurs when in his narrative Hawkins refers to the 'black spot', given to Silver to depose him from his position as pirate captain. Hawkins tells us that 'I have that curiosity beside me at this moment; but not a trace of writing now remains beyond a single scratch' (162). This piece of paper is known in theoretical terms as a palimpsest – underneath the fading black spot lies another arch-narrative, namely the Bible: the original gospel has been overwritten by a pirate message, calling into question the sacrosanct authority of the original text and the problems of Gospel Truth. This palimpsest (a piece of writing that is hidden beneath another written work) serves as a paradigm for the entire novel in the sense that both in terms of form and content, there is a continual oscillation between a surface claim and a counter-claim lying beneath. It further demonstrates the tension between realism and modernism in the text, or between prelapsarian childhood and postlapsarian adulthood. Hawkins reaches a level of experiential knowledge in the text, when he learns not to trust the word of Long John Silver, not to take him at face value, when that face is always a concealing mask. His awakening from innocence to experience takes place in the apple barrel, with its connotations of Eve and the tree of knowledge. But Treasure Island is not the Edenic space portrayed in Ballantyne's vision of South Sea paradise. 'Jim Hawkins is caught between emotional and imaginative attraction to the exotic and value-free world' of Silver, yet also drawn to the 'sensible appreciation of the essential order and decency of Squire Trelawny and Dr Livesey' (Gifford et al. 2002: 403). Trelawny and Livesey are not decent, though – the earlier quote about 'money to eat' indicates merely a façade of respectability.

In Ballantyne's novel, the desert island conveyed a motif of Edenic innocent space, to be filled with Western childhood and the message of civilization's enlightenment. Stevenson's text, on the other hand, tends to parody this notion of paradise, offering instead an anti-Edenic space. On reaching the island, Jim builds up a picture of the atmosphere that pervades the scene, saying 'perhaps it was the look of the island, with its grey, melancholy woods, and wild stone spires [. . .] my heart sank, as the saying is, into my boots; and from that first look onward, I hated the very thought of Treasure Island' (68–9), 'The heat was sweltering, and the men grumbled fiercely over their work' (69), and 'There was not a breath of air moving [. . .] A peculiar stagnant smell hung over the anchorage – a smell of sodden leaves and rotting tree trunks' (70). The geographical and climatic composition of the island is intertwined with the mutinous behaviour of the crew who, of course, are pirates and would have mutinied anyway. Jim tells us, 'If the conduct of the men had been alarming in the boat, it became truly threatening when they had come aboard [. . .] Mutiny, it was plain, hung over us like a thunder-cloud' (70). Using pathetic fallacy, inner psyche is mingled with outer climate to form an ominous duality in which thundery tempers align with thunderous weather. Treasure Island is described as a stagnant place of decomposition and decay which itself mirrors the inner corruption played out by the pirates in their unquenchable thirst for treasure. Converging landscape and mindscape, 'As an image of the fully integrated self, the island is often an earthly paradise' (Blackburn 1983: 9) – be it Avalon, the Isles of the Blessed, or the Garden of Eden. As 'Paradise is, imaginatively if not literally, an island', it therefore functions as 'an image of the self' (Blackburn 1983: 9). Clearly, though, Stevenson is not deploying this metaphorical use of the island landscape to capture a sense of innocence, but, instead, to convey an inner corruption at the heart of the pirates' pursuit of 'pieces of eight', for 'The island setting, then, from Defore on, serves as an archetypal laboratory for a society's ideology' (Maher 1988: 169).

The ideology that Stevenson's imaginative island is probing is that of the British Empire and its colonial enterprise. Stripped of Ballantyne's legitimizers, such as Christianity and cannibalism, Stevenson's novel inverts the position of Western intervention by displaying only the bare, skeletal location of wealth (referred to as 'skeleton island') in a fiction whose very title smacks of nothing but profit that strips the island to the bone. In literature, 'The island, from Shakespeare's *The Tempest* onwards, has provided the European imagination with an ideal sense of instruction. On islands – geographically sealed-off units – there is the possibility of representing colonial dreams and fears in miniature' (Bristow 1991: 94). Often in children's literature the island serves as a microcosmic world where dangers can be explored within safe boundaries, allowing 'Boy heroes' to 'act as the natural masters of these controllable environments' (Bristow 1991: 94). As such, 'Islands can provide an appositely "child-like" space which boys can easily circumnavigate without revealing any lack of manful maturity' (Bristow 1991: 94). As islands, if populated at all, are peopled 'only by savages', they are represented as being 'racially inferior' and, thus, 'ultimately prove no threat to the boys who occupy this territory' (Bristow 1991: 94). While much of Bristow's comments support a reading of *The Coral Island*, *Treasure Island* remains ambiguously problematic, falling more into the 'colonial fears' than 'hopes' category and the savage inhabitant is a Westerner. The island space itself becomes as significant a storyteller of events than any of the characters, for 'The chill and the vapour taken together told a poor tale of the island. It was plainly a damp, feverish, unhealthy spot' (104). What is unearthed or brought to the surface is that pervious colonial representations of Western intervention as Edenic are a mask which belies the truth of Empire expansion and economic gain. The English arrival on Treasure Island does not transform it into a Christian paradise but attaches it with the significance of Western market value: it is labelled and perceived as an island of treasure by the 'gentlemen of fortune' who have charted a course to its shores.

In two senses, the island tells a 'poor tale' – on the one hand because the gentlemen of fortune behave exploitatively against the feminine landscape and, on the other, because the island is impoverished by such intervention. Although the island's humidity is linked with the pirate mutiny, it is also entwined with the other camp in this treasure hunt, those so-called respectable 'gentlemen of fortune' who, on the one hand, denounce the pirate's greed, yet simultaneously desire to line their own pockets. Squire Trelawny hypocritically claims, 'I'll have that treasure if I search a year' (32) and 'We'll have [. . .] money to eat' (34). The map they pore over is 'shaped, you might say, like a fat dragon' (34) according to Jim and the implication is that the chivalrous Christian knights of old are setting out to slay the dragon, or to dig up the feminine landscape in the masculine aggression of Empire. Just as the Squire admires the bloodthirsty exploits of the infamous pirate, Captain Flint, we are reminded in the text that upon such men's shoulders does the greatness of England depend. As well as the far-flung colonies of the globe, 'Perhaps in *Treasure Island*, the island may figure as Ireland (a colony), as much as it represents a realm of far-off plunder' (Bristow 1991: 121).

Having considered the journey of the characters as representing a colonial process emanating from British patriarchy, it is worth considering the Oedipal father-figures. Billy Bones, though a violent pirate, is someone whom Jim Hawkins is simultaneously terrified of and drawn to. As storyteller, Bones both represents grotesque nightmare and seductive allure, someone who intrigues Jim. When he dies, Hawkins tells us that 'as soon as I saw that he was dead, I burst into a flood of tears' (18), apparently more moved and traumatized by the demise of this criminal than he is by the death of his own father, which receives only scant reference. Clearly, both deaths are linked in Jim's mind but the floodgates only seem to open when this relative stranger passes out of his life. Another character who oozes terror yet also entices the narrator is Pew, who

> was plainly blind, for he tapped before him with a stick [. . .]
> and he was hunched [. . .] and wore a huge old tattered sea-cloak
> with a hood, that made him appear positively deformed. I never
> saw in my life a more dreadful looking figure [. . .] I held out my
> hand, and the horrible, soft-spoken, eyeless creature gripped it
> in a moment like a vice. (16)

Although Pew is a hunchback, deformed Gothic nightmare, the presumed innocent child-figure offers him his hand to hold, which is immediately gripped in a sinister fashion.

The most powerful and seductive father figure is the arch-deceiver Long John Silver, who creates a familial tie with Jim Hawkins by alluding to him as the 'picter of my own self when I was young and handsome' (150). It is Silver who has imprinted himself upon the mind of the narrator: on the final page of the novel, he says 'Of Silver we have heard no more. That formidable seafaring man with one leg has at last gone clean out of my life' (191). But as this novel demonstrates, a doubleness in its Victorian realist format set against the approaching onslaught of modernism, the ending of the text does not offer linear closure. Instead, this is a cyclical text, where the narrative thread spirals back from the end to the beginning in complicated loops, not straight lines. Thus, in the opening stages of the novel, Jim confesses, 'How that personage haunted my dreams, I need scarcely tell you' (3). The inference, then, is not that Silver has gone clean out of Jim's life, but has actually left an indelible mark in the narrator's psyche, which is forever played out in the (re)telling of the tale. Jim's haunting narrative continues,

> I would see him in a thousand forms, and with a thousand dia-bolical expressions. Now the leg would be cut off at the knee, now at the hip; now he was a monstrous kind of a creature who had never had but the one leg, and that in the middle of his body. To see him leap and run and pursue me over hedge and ditch was the worst of nightmares. (3)

Through Jim's imagination, before even meeting Silver, a feeling of terror is evoked, as he imagines being stalked by a maimed, grotesque, yet simultaneously seductive figure. This 'monstrous creature' whose leg is 'in the middle of his body' metaphorically suggests an erect phallus which is in pursuit of Jim's innocence. The terrifying erotic image of Silver that haunts the narrator's dreams is played out through the safe distancing technique of displacement onto another character. In a parodic act of sodomy, Tom is murdered by Silver when they reach Treasure Island, witnessed at a safe distance by Jim: 'Silver, agile as a monkey, even without leg or crutch, was on the top of him next moment, and had twice buried his knife up to the hilt in that defenceless body. From my place of ambush, I could hear him pant aloud as he struck the blows' (76). The murder assumes a dimension of rape, where Silver is heard to 'pant aloud' at the climactic point of death, after burying his phallically symbolic knife up to the hilt in Tom's feminized 'defenceless body'.

Silver as a lower-class Other is also referred to in Social–Darwinist terminology as being 'agile as a monkey' (there are echoes of *Jekyll and Hyde*, where Mr Hyde is described in primate terminology). Silver's deformity adds to his monstrous capacity to impose an air of menace. The father-figures of Pew and Billy Bones are equally described in such monstrous terms – Pew is blind, hunchbacked and wearing a cloak (a bit like the Grim-Reaper, perhaps), and Bones becomes a debilitated figure, having had a stroke and later becomes a corpse through alcohol abuse. The novel contains an Oedipal drama and the debilitated pirates represent castration fears. The younger generation, represented through Jim, are always waiting to depose the older generation of father-figures in society (modernism sought to "make it new" and sweep away the traditions of Victorian patriarchal realism). Yet, fear emanates from Jim as he moves from innocence to experience where, in the apple barrel, he learns about the deceptive doubleness of language and individuals. Jim's biological father who remains offstage is very quickly killed off, replaced by the son. Jim overturns the adult/child power structure and tends to infantilize his mother who, in stereotypical gendered fashion, faints at the first sight of trouble. Being pursued by the murderous pirates, Jim informs us that

> I blamed my poor mother for her honesty and her greed, for her past foolhardiness and present weakness [. . .] sure enough, she gave a sigh and fell on my shoulder. I do not know how I found the strength to do it all, and I am afraid it was roughly done; but I managed to drag her down the bank. (23–4)

As well as seeing these monstrous figures as Oedipal fathers, they can also be viewed as a potential erotic postlapsarian threat to the perceived prelapsarian purity of childhood. Stevenson's novel, in that light, could be playing out the dramatic tension that exists within adult culture and its desire to create an innocent space called childhood, when all the time that innocence contains the mask of postlapsarian construction. This problematic dual level that exists in children's literature between adult creator and child reader can have erotic dimensions, as is considered by James Kincaid's *Child-Loving* which questions this preoccupation with the normalizing and revering of innocence. Or Jacqueline Rose suggests that children's fiction is 'something of a soliciting, a chase, or even a seduction', for 'when children's fiction touches on that barrier, it becomes not experiment [. . .] but *molestation*' (Rose 1994: 70). Consider, too, the dramatic chase that ensues between the pirate Israel Hands and Jim, who is threatened by a phallic penetrative knife.

Silver's parrot acquires fictional dimensions, regarded by the ultimate storyteller, Silver, to 'may be, two hundred years old' (54). The parrot's voice is significant – it provides the double-edge that lurks beneath the façade of Silver's deceptive flattering language. The bird voices the gap that exists between Silver's words and the concealed truth beneath them, though it is ironically incapable of deciphering the hieroglyphics of Western discourse in order to detect the truth about what it speaks. A dual meaning is attached to parrot in the text: on the one hand, it refers immediately to Silver's parrot, itself a double as it is named after the pirate Cap'n Flint (so it performs an identity). On the other hand, to parrot in the text means to 'blab', as 'the secret has been told to the parrot' 'Silver's parrot?' asked the squire. 'It's a way of speaking,' said the captain. 'Blabbed, I mean' (48). Silver's parrot effectively blabs the truth about Silver's misdeeds. The ultimate lie which the parrot blabs or brings to the surface from its concealed depths, is the truth behind colonial enterprise which, is to extract 'Pieces of eight! pieces of eight!' (191) from an island that is seen only in economic stature as being composed of treasure. The man of the island, Ben Gunn, described by Hawkins as 'a white man like myself' (79), replaces boy's adventure stories like Ballantyne's who included savage cannibals, and suggests the Other lurks not externally, but internally within the self. For Oscar Wilde, the greatest fear in Victorian morality is that they will see 'Caliban's face in the mirror' reflected back at them – Squire Trelawny's cannibalistic desire to have 'money to eat' certainly reflects this.

L. FRANK BAUM – *THE WONDERFUL WIZARD OF OZ* (1900)

In considering the works of fantasy below (and *Alice*), simultaneously consult the fantasy theorists mentioned in Chapter 4. When L. Frank Baum's *The Wonderful Wizard of Oz* was published in 1900, it was an instant success with its child readership, though not so with its adult critics. It was only fairly recently that the novel was seriously considered and, at times, it suffers similar condemnations that J.K. Rowling's books have faced. Alison Lurie tells us that 'Fundamentalist Christians have complained that *The Wizard of Oz* contains two good witches (to them, an oxymoron) and also that, "in Oz, females assume traditional male roles, and animals are elevated to human status."' (Lurie 2003: 45). Those who believe in creationism, argues Lurie, regard such characters as the Cowardly Lion, who speak and give advice to humans, as 'a serious threat' (Lurie 2003: 45). Children's fantasy writing arose in Britain with a revival of interest in fairy tales in the nineteenth century, defending the rights of the imagination and challenging those who revere instilling facts into children's minds. Baum wrote in his Introduction that traditional fairy tales needed to be updated: 'the time has come for a series of newer "wonder tales" in which the stereotyped genie, dwarf and fairy are eliminated [. . .] "The Wonderful Wizard of Oz" was written solely to pleasure children of to-day'. Whether that intention of pure pleasure bears out, though, is up for contention because, arguably, the novel is full of dark elements and uncertainties. Often in children's fantasy, the secondary or fantasy world is framed by a more recognizable primary world, as with *Alice*. In *The Wonderful Wizard of Oz* (this was later shortened to *The Wizard of Oz*), the fantasy realm of Oz is framed by the outer familiarity of Kansas. Peter Hunt says, 'characters from "our" world enter or leave the other worlds, thus keeping them in perspective' (Hunt 1994: 185). Further, in children's fantasy, the child hero tends to carry out acts that empower them while, in society, children are otherwise disempowered and so would identify with the hero or heroine.

Baum had a heart defect – interestingly, the Tin Woodman desires the Wizard of Oz to give him a heart. Because of his heart defect, Baum spent much of his childhood time reading rather than participating in physical games, developing a love of fiction in his formative years (Stevenson's childhood was also plagued with illness). In 1881, he fell in love with Maud Gage, daughter of one of America's most well-known early radical feminists, Matilda Gage, who co-wrote the *History of Woman Suffrage* (1881–89). He married Maud in November 1882. Due to such strong feminist influence, Baum was a supporter of women's rights in America, and critics have argued that Dorothy in *The Wizard of Oz* is an embodiment of American female pioneering strength and determination

(Victor Fleming's cinematic version of *The Wizard of Oz* in 1939 portrays what is critically regarded to be a considerably weaker female heroine – see Mark I. West's 'The Dorothy's of Oz: A Heroine's Unmaking' in Butts (ed.), *Stories and Society: Children's Literature in its Social Context*, 1992). *Oz* was Baum's greatest literary success: he published 13 sequels and, following his death, other authors continued to write stories about Oz.

With a framed narrative, in which the secondary unknown world is surrounded by a primary recognizable domain, the reader is assured that there is a safe returnable world for the hero or heroine, but it also creates a dichotomy between here and there, the recognizable and the unknown, where the latter tends to involve exotic, yet potentially dangerous elements. The primary world in *The Wizard of Oz* is first encountered, set in the so-called real world of Kansas (but that, too, is a fictional representation/re-presentation of Kansas). The description is so negative that anyone might want to escape from it. Bleakness and sterility dominate the landscape, which even manages to infiltrate and drain the home domain and its inhabitants, culminating in a lack of domestic bliss and familial affection. The dichotomy of this landscape is Oz, where Dorothy arrives

> in the midst of a country of marvellous beauty. There were lovely patches of greensward all about, with stately trees bearing rich and luscious fruit. Banks of gorgeous flowers were on every hand, and birds with rare and brilliant plumage sang and fluttered in the trees and bushes. A little way off was a small brook, rushing and sparkling along between green banks, and murmuring a voice very grateful to a little girl who had lived so long on the dry, grey prairies. (9)

The contrast is from scarcity to plenitude, from sterility to fertility, in a fantasy world of growth, song and the quenching of one's thirsts and hunger drives. The juxtaposition of 'the great Kansas prairies' and 'Their house was small' (5) emphasizes the claustrophobic feeling of being trapped in an eternal wasteland. The individual is dwarfed by the vastness of the flat dustbowl at their feet. 'When Dorothy stood in the doorway and looked around, she could see nothing but the great gray prairie on every side. Not a tree nor a house broke the broad sweep of flat country that reached to the edge of the sky in all directions' (5). Life-blood is drained away from this landscape: 'The sun had baked the ploughed land into a grey mass, with little cracks running through it. Even the grass was not green, for the sun had burned the tops of the long blades until they were the same grey colour to be seen everywhere. Once the house had been painted, but the sun blistered the paint and rains washed it away, and now the house was as dull and grey as everything else' (5–6). This panoramic narrative gaze casts around at the vast void of terrain, panning closer until we see the human dimension and oppression by the elements. The repetitive references to the colour grey indicate a lifeless, soulless environment where inspiration literally drains away.

The grey exterior canvas shifts to the inhabitants' interior living space, until they become indistinguishable from it. They are alive but have ceased to enjoy life's pleasures: demonstrations of love and joy are thwarted, leaving only shells or shadows of humanity behind. This striking imagery anticipates F. Scott Fitzgerald's *The Great Gatsby* (1925), with its poverty-stricken area the 'Valley of Ashes' populated by 'ash-grey men' who move soullessly as though already dead. Both of these American novels evoke exhaustion at the overwhelming pressure of succeeding in the American Dream. Such American optimism is not allowed to take root in Baum's representation of the Kansas frontier. It has dramatically affected Dorothy's aunt, for

> When Aunt Em came there to live she was a young, pretty wife. The sun and wind had changed her, too. They had taken the sparkle from her eyes and left them a sober grey; they had taken the red from her cheeks and lips, and they were grey also. She was thin and gaunt, and never smiled now. (6)

Aunt Em's youthful identity is robbed by the harsh environment of which she has become a part, and the marriage of responsibility into which she has entered. If eyes are the windows to the soul, then Aunt Em is frozen in her grey sterility, incapable of feeling or emanating any kind of desire for life. But she is not the only one locked into this miserable existence, because 'Uncle Henry never laughed. He worked hard from morning till night and did not know what joy was' (6). Trying to eke out an existence amid this harsh landscape has left its imprint upon the very faces of these characters, almost like the cracks in the clay of the sun-baked prairie. Historically, 'Pioneer farmers toward the end of the century were experiencing many and drastic changes', including rapid railway expansion between 1870 and 1880, which 'stimulated the rapid increase in population of new settlers on the frontier' (Junko in McGillis 2003: 157–68). Notably, Kansas was the site of 'excessive cultivation of farmland. Then the drought in 1887 caused serious damages to the agricultural products in west Kansas [. . .] During four years after 1887, half of the pioneer farmers left Kansas' (Junko 2003: 161). As a criticism of the American Dream, the search for the yellow brick streets paved with gold through hard work proves a sham, just like the Wizard who lacks substance or credibility. No matter how hard Uncle Henry and Aunt Em work, their surroundings still remain harsh with little reward, and their lives a continual struggle against the elements. The American Dream, then, seems to be a false prophet: America's land of the so-called free was built upon the Protestant work ethic of Puritanism, self-sacrifice and toil. Perhaps it is pertinent that the china object smashed by the Lion is a church. The Wizard of Oz himself wields a God-like influence in which his people are in awe, never having seen him, yet exposed by the text to be 'a humbug'. According to Henry M. Littlefield (1964), the silver shoes with the magical powers to solve Dorothy's dilemma, symbolize the silver standard, serving as an allegory for the Populist Party's belief that silver would solve the problems facing farmers. Populism supported the common people. Like many people, however, Dorothy does not understand the power she possesses, but she sets out on the yellow brick road, symbolizing the gold standard, which proves to be a perilous journey. She finally learns of their power at the end of the story, but the shoes are lost when Dorothy returns home. With the decline of the Populist Party, the demand for the free coinage of silver also faded as a national issue.

As a child, Dorothy does not have much to laugh about, reared in this place with a cold, reserved aunt and uncle. Dorothy is an orphan figure, literally homeless and without roots – it is no wonder that she spends the entire novel searching for home. Further, as children's literature and childhood offer a redemptive source for adult society, it is hardly surprising that she sounds a discordant note of hope in this otherwise bleak existence. As the child heroine, she brings the only bit of colour to this dreary Kansas landscape – she is not grey and neither is the source of her pleasure,

Toto. Hence, the child's psyche is Oz, dramatized in the Technicolor of the movie. Em is what Dorothy will potentially become without Oz. Junko believes that it is only Dorothy's aunt and uncle who are 'exhausted with the greyness and the hardships of pioneer life. There is no mention of Dorothy being actually overwhelmed by the greyness' (Junko 2003: 159). Rather, Junko regards Dorothy as 'a pleasant and innocent girl whose cheerfulness is protected by Toto. She represents the happiness, innocence, and hope that Aunt Em and Uncle Henry have lost in the course of their pioneer lives' (Junko 2003: 159). I would partially agree, but in Dorothy's unconscious psyche she is alienated and lacking, which spurs the fantasy journey – otherwise, Dorothy, too, will be diminished by her surroundings. It is precisely *because* Dorothy is overwhelmed that she cannot verbalize her loneliness and frustration within the confines of the symbolic order: the storm is her semiotic language that transports her to the other side of the rainbow. The setting resonates of an existence on America's hinterlands or margins – being transplanted here as an orphan, Dorothy is located geographically and psychologically on the outskirts of life. The storm brewing, therefore, assumes an inner as well as meteorological significance that transports Dorothy to a fantasy realm of colour, plenitude and fertility, accompanied by Toto, the only piece of colour in the primary dimension that brings her joy. Although at no point in the opening stages of the novel does Dorothy voice a desire to escape the grey Kansas prairie, nevertheless it is clear that there is an inner desire not uttered in language, but through the more feminine or imaginary domain of the storm. She is accompanied by the very thing she inwardly wishes to escape from, namely her adopted home and immediately sets out on a quest to return to it, arguing when she reaches Oz that, 'There's no place like home' (25). Glinda says that she could have 'gone back to your Aunt Em the very first day you came to this country' (157). Had she done so, there would be little story and Dorothy needed to search for what was always there, but not necessarily recognized or valued at the time. The home that she is dissatisfied with must undergo a transformation within the colourful realm of Oz, just as Dorothy, too, is altered by the journey.

As an orphan, she experiences, in Freudian terminology, an Oedipal crisis because she lacks a pre-Oedipal bond with the mother and initially this is not compensated for by the surrogate mother figure, Aunt Em. Dorothy's quest to return home to Kansas, then, is not just a physical journey but also entails a desire to return to a reconstituted Aunt Em, from whom Dorothy desires love and nurturing. In the Kansas before Dorothy journeys to Oz, there are multiple images of deprivation and hunger, paralleled with a continual plenitude of eating (with the occasional fear of hunger) in the fantasy realm. For example, 'Dorothy ate a hearty supper' (18), 'she ate a hearty breakfast' (19) and she 'breakfasted like a princess off peaches and plums from the trees beside the river' (50). The pre-Oedipal association with a desire for the security of the absent mother is clearly established during the cyclone, which offers a metaphorical protective womb for Dorothy during the external chaos of the storm: 'she felt as if she were being rocked gently, like a baby in a cradle' (7). As a psychological rupture, the storm is as much a part of Dorothy's unfulfilled desires as it is a meteorological phenomenon: her name is Dorothy Gale and she rages internally with the same torrent that transports her over the rainbow.

The journey upon which Dorothy embarks is towards the Emerald City, located at the centre of Oz, with the premise that she will discover a Great Wizard who can fulfil her wish to return home. Her mindscape/landscape route along the yellow-brick road leads her to a centre that is hollow because the Wizard is a fraud. Gold brick is slang terminology for something worthless with only a surface appearance of value, and is a sham or a fraud while, during the California Gold Rush (1848–55), fool's gold or iron pyrites was often mistaken for gold. Dorothy learns that she herself holds the power of returning, while the wizard conveys the blind faith of ideological manipulation and cannot materialize that which she craves – he disappears full of hot air in a balloon. Structurally, Dorothy's journey to the centre of Oz is also roughly the centre of the novel. When she reaches that central point, her journey spirals her back towards her starting point, so the novel ends circularly where it began. But because she has embarked upon a journey, home is, by necessity, altered – it is now somewhere she can be content – in her absence the longed-for mother figure of Aunt Em has re-discovered her capacity to love. She emphatically greets Dorothy as 'My darling child!', 'covering her face with kisses' (160). Dorothy now has ownership in an invested mother figure as Em claims her as her own, thus fixing Dorothy's desires in her domestic terrain. As child heroine, she has also returned some colour to the drab adult habitation, returning adult culture to a co-existence with the needs of childhood fantasy. The hope is that Dorothy's quest for fulfilled desire will have altered things sufficiently that she will not follow in Aunt Em's footsteps – remember when Em first arrived in Kansas she, like Dorothy, was high spirited, but became drained of colour. The psychological storm generated by Dorothy Gale's unhappiness, then, transports her on a journey that directly alters her relationship with home.

Unlike the conventional recognizable realm of the symbolic order, Oz exists as a kind of feminine disruption of that real world, providing a space in which inner unconscious pre-Oedipal anxieties and desires can be played out. That is why during her first arrival in the fantasy realm, a witch tells Dorothy that, although Kansas has no witches, 'you see, the Land of Oz has never been civilized, for we are cut off from all the rest of the world' (12). Unlike the repressive standards and encroachments of the civilized world, the fantasy dimension of Oz is free of such constraints – it is a fluid place where one's inner self can be explored. But, fantasy, like the unconscious, is a complex mixture of light and darkness, representing desires and anxieties, so Dorothy learns that, 'It is a long journey, through a country that is sometimes pleasant and sometimes dark and terrible' (14) and, 'The country here is rich and pleasant, but you must pass through rough and dangerous places before you reach the end of your journey' (19). Part of that journey, like many children's texts, involves passing through a forest, symbolizing darkness, danger and erotic threats lurking beyond the safe parameters of home, though this is the place that the Lion feels most at home in. Each character's sense of home, therefore, oscillates between civilized and untamed and what is familiar to one will be uncanny to another. Dorothy's abrupt return scene to Kansas has been regarded as being problematic in its relative shortness by some critics. Regardless, the return does follow a typical pattern in children's literature of the home-journey-home structure, and, like the cyclone, Dorothy's quest follows a circular movement back to her original position. But home is a new home that has been built in her absence, suggesting the potential for new beginnings and feelings of belonging. The Silver Shoes are 'lost for ever in the desert' (159), signalling that Dorothy's wanderlust days are behind her as she settles into her renegotiated surroundings. Her relationship with the desired mother figure in the text is also replenished in a new forged feminine alliance with Aunt Em, whose own development has extended to the landscape, where cabbages are growing and water is available. The growing grass further suggests a fertile landscape comparable with the ravished scorched earth in the opening sequences of the narrative. Although she falls asleep during the cyclone, unlike the film version, the novel does not confirm that Dorothy was dreaming – the cinematic story awakens her from a dream, but Baum's text describes a physical return as 'she rolled over upon the grass several times' (159).

Baum's support of feminism often leads critics to regard Dorothy as a popular strong pioneering female character, who actively sets out on an adventure: 'Unlike all the other American children's fiction of the period – series books, boys' adventure tales, girls' domestic novels – the Oz stories appealed to both boys and girls'. (Murray 1998: 100–4) Dorothy 'embodie[s] both feminine virtues (compassion, kindness, acceptance of those different from herself, concern for others' feelings) and masculine attributes (rationality, assertiveness, single-mindedness, courage, perseverance)' (Murray 1998: 100–4). The idea of perception in the Emerald City is significant, for 'Everyone *seemed* happy and contented and prosperous' (70, my italics). This misperception is caused by wearing green-tinted spectacles. The Wizard says, '[T]o make the name fit better I put green spectacles on all the people, so that everything they saw was green' (116) but, ultimately he confesses, 'I have been making believe' (113), signalling that he has created a fantasy. Meanwhile, the theme of slavery is explored: the winged monkeys and the yellow guards are finally set free from their lives of enslavement, while the Wicked Witch of the West also makes Dorothy her domestic slave. The monkey leader says that 'Once [. . .] we were a free people, living happily in the great forest, flying from tree to tree, eating nuts and fruit, and doing just as we pleased without calling anyone master [. . .] many years ago, long before Oz came out of the clouds to rule over this land' (105). Released when Dorothy kills the Wicked Witch of the West, nevertheless this suggests that the Wizard's ideology has created social divisions through his sham 'rule' (113).

FRANCES HODGSON BURNETT – *THE SECRET GARDEN* (1911)

The association made between child and garden in forming an integral part of the discourse of childhood innocence is integral to

Frances Hodgson Burnett's *The Secret Garden*. The influence of Romantic discourse upon childhood perceives the child as being closer to Nature and capable, in turn, of maintaining an unchanging prelapsarian space in which adult society can find refuge. These themes are very important in Burnett's novel, first published in 1911. Two of the most prominent advocates of the relationship between childhood and nature are Jean-Jacques Rousseau and Friedrich Froebel, and their influence in *The Secret Garden* is worth considering (indeed, their legacy can been traced even to more contemporary Western children's literature). Froebel writes in his book, *Pedagogics of the Kindergarten*, that, 'The word kindergarten [or . . .] *the garden of the children*' is an absolute cultural as well as spiritual necessity. He continues,

> a garden of the children [. . .] proceeds not only from the higher reason just given [i.e. spiritual nurturance], but also from reasons of social and citizen collective life. The human being, the child, as a part of humanity must even early not only be recognized and treated as individual and single, but must recognize itself as such and prove itself to be such by its action. But this reciprocal activity between one and a few, a part and a whole, is nowhere more beautifully, vividly, and definitely expressed than in the associated cultivation of plants, the common care of a garden [. . .] representing the relation of the particular to the general, of the part to the whole, of the child to the family, of the citizen to the community. (Froebel, 1899: 218–19)

Froebel applies the garden as a tool in which the child can be cultivated towards recognizing its own position and the part it is expected to play in society. This message resonates throughout Burnett's text when Mary and Colin (both unruly and highly self-centred children) are shifted from a position of isolation towards communal enterprise, through the quasi-mystical 'healing' powers of the secret garden which they unearth. Froebel's theory was widely embraced in Victorian and Edwardian society, where the focus upon childhood as an ideal state was becoming ever prominent. The view was taken that children's innocence could best be cultivated and preserved within nature, with the connotations with Eden as a site of prelapsarian bliss. In children's fiction, pastoral spaces like the garden or the island function in this way. Rousseau writes in *Emile*, his treatise on education that,

> Cities are the abyss of the human species. At the end of a few generations the races perish or degenerate. They must be renewed, and it is always the country which provides for this renewal. Send your children, then, to renew themselves, as it were, and to regain in the midst of the fields the vigor that is lost in the unhealthy air of overpopulated places. (Rousseau 1979 [1762]: 59)

The language employed by both Rousseau and Froebel uses horticultural terminology to provide a metaphor for the rearing of children – thus, children themselves become akin to plants – both require fresh air, and a suitable environmental space to be able to develop 'normally', as witnessed in the transformation of Mary and Colin from a position of stunted, withering confinement (both in terms of Colin's suffocating bedroom and Mary's stifling India) towards an altogether healthier, thriving development.

The sense of community that Froebel advocates as being an integral part of the garden's influence upon the child is mirrored in the advice proffered by Dickon's mother in the novel. She philosophizes that

> When I was at school my jography told as th' world was shaped like a orange an' I found out [. . .] that th' whole orange doesn't belong to nobody [. . .] What children learns from children [. . .] is that there's no sense in grabbin' at th' whole orange – peel an' all. If you do, you'll likely not even get th' pips, an' them's too bitter to eat. (195–6)

Note the rustic language spoken by Mother Sowerby, as the text strives to link her lower-class rustic status with a kind of peasant honesty, raising questions about the representation of social class in the novel, and whether it ultimately upholds dominant ideologies of the time? Mother Sowerby says that children learn as part of their socialization process that they only own part of the world and it does not revolve entirely around them, in the sense that they move from their infant state of egocentrism towards social interaction. Each future citizen, then, is familiarized with their social ranking in a way that echoes Froebel's concepts. This tendency to equate childhood with nature is fraught with contradictions. If childhood is supposed to be inherently innocent and interlinked with nature, why does there appear to be a requirement to instil this from external influences? Gardens themselves are not natural environments but, on the contrary, highly constructed, artificial spaces. Though childhood and gardens are perceived to be natural and pure in their prelapsarian facets, ironically, both are subject to cultural manipulation from postlapsarian society. At the time when the text was published, efforts were being made in British society to provide city gardens in order to help to bring such influences to bear upon children from urban, lower class backgrounds. As the early beginnings of a Welfare State were emerging, working-class children were becoming increasingly a focus of social intervention (such as the introduction of free school meals for poorer children in 1906).

Influenced by Froebel's theories, 'the famous nineteenth-century proponent of the kindergarten, McMillan – in 1911, the year in which *The Secret Garden* was published – established a "camp school" (i.e., a city garden) for the sick and impoverished children of Deptford, South London' (Phillips 1993: 177). This camp school sought to provide a pastoral haven that could 'counter the spiritual deficits of urban working-class childhood' by attempting to 'realize the organic unity [. . .] that allegedly existed between the child and the natural world' (Phillips 1993: 177). This served to remedy the negative impact of urban squalor through 'a transcendent moral aesthetic – that of nature itself' (Phillips 1993: 177), given the therapeutic associations with gardens. It would also serve to 'rescue culture from political controversy, even from national decline [. . .] the urban garden was not only called upon to take the slum out of the working-class child, it also set the task of building fit bodies and keeping the bulldog spirit in place' (Phillips 1993: 178). This is a social implementation influenced by Rousseau, who argued, 'I want to raise Emile in the country far from [. . .] the black morals of cities which are covered with a veneer seductive and contagious for children' (Rousseau 1991 [1762]: 95). Although not working-class, nevertheless Burnett's characters, Mary and Colin, are in desperate need of the healing powers of the secret garden which saves them both. Phillips recognizes the Social Darwinism that is aligned with child and garden (evident in relation to boy's adventure stories and colonial pursuits at the height of the British Empire). Part of the motif that Burnett's novel employs is the concept of a sick, weakened body and spirit – Colin is crippled and Mary is suffering from the debilitating influences of colonial India: both are poignantly healed through specifically English fresh air. Rousseau similarly refers to 'black morals' (this is a polar binary of black and white, as the cultural Other is described in darkened terms – be it, for instance, darkest Africa, the contagion of working-class sexual proliferation, in darkest England, and the resultant need to maintain the purity of British superiority). Colin very pointedly states, 'I shall stop being queer [. . .] if I go every day to the garden' (235). Through a regime of fresh air and gardening, Colin vows that his queer behaviour (in the sense that it does not accord with notions of idealized childhood, though also with effeminate possibilities) will cease and he will be normalized into the cultural construction of the child he ought to be. The working-class Dickon, significantly raised on the Yorkshire Moors, is represented in his purest, almost primitive form, as opposed to the corrupt urban world that surrounds, for instance, Oliver Twist in Dickensian London.

A third dimension which plays a crucial role in this child/garden equation is the figure of the Mother, particularly Dickon's Mother, Susan Sowerby, who is continually alluded to as Mother. The basis of such a relationship can be found in Froebel's patriarchal discourse about the kindergarten. He says, 'the mother must take care that the child develops in union with Nature and in contrast with it' (Froebel 1899: 309). Apparently,

> Through such fostering she (the mother) appears pre-eminently in her true nature, her real position, and in her manifold and, to the child, important connections, for first she stands as a connecting link between her child and his Creator, the Original Source of his life – God. Next she connects the child with her husband, his earthly father. She is the link that joins the child with the family of which he is a member. Through the family she unites the child to the human race, with humanity, and with each individual member of humanity [. . .] Finally, and lastly, and in a special sense, she is the bond of union between the child and Nature. (Froebel 1899: 307)

Such discourses, then, place not only the child but also the Mother into the terrain of the garden, linking the mother with Mother Earth/ Nature as the nurturer of mankind. In *The Secret Garden*, Susan Sowerby is closely aligned with the rustic environment, and yet at the same time she is the domesticated Angel in the House figure of patriarchal discourse in her role as nurturing mother. She plays an integral role in the socialization of contrary Mary and her hysterical cousin, Colin, guiding them away from being contrary and queer towards a path of cultural purity. Susan Sowerby is paralleled with Mary's mother, Mrs Lennox, who is portrayed as a negative, unnatural mother insofar as she is a socialite, who has little time for her daughter and, instead, employs a maid to look after her. As the narrative, focalized from Mary's perspective, observes, Susan Sowerby 'doesn't seem to be like the mothers in India' (87). The lack which Mary experiences in early childhood at the pre-Oedipal stage, when, according to psychoanalytic theory, the child is most closely unified with the mother, is immediately pointed, for

> her mother had been a great beauty who cared only to go to parties and amuse herself with gay people. She had not wanted a little girl at all, and when Mary was born she handed her over to the care of an Ayah, who was made to understand that if she wished to please the Memsahib she must keep the child out of sight as much as possible. (1)

As well as the Indian air and environment failing to nurture Mary, even her mother discards her because of her gender inferiority in a patriarchal society. Representing colonial discourse, Mary's Anglo–Indian displacement is seen to be negative to her development. The garden that Mary tries to grow in India fails to develop, as everything is subject to an oppressive environment. Compared with the nursery rhyme, 'Mistress Mary, quite contrary, how does your garden grow?' (9), only her return home (where she has never been before) to England counteracts her contrariness. Mike Cadden refers to this position of home and alien land in Burnett's novel in the way that 'home is linked to racial essentialism' and 'to issues of blood; the concept of blood, in turn, is represented through the metaphors of magic and disease [. . .] that mark the essential and insuperable divisions between cultures' (Cadden 1997: 55). *The Secret Garden* regards "home" as 'not necessarily the house in which one was born and raised; "home" is the home of one's people' (Cadden 1997: 55). Mary's 'change in setting from India to England' is described 'as a return home despite the fact that Mary has never before lived in England' (Cadden 1997: 55). Colin, too, shows signs of degeneration and sickness through his unhealthy confinement indoors in a feminine space and it is only in the outdoor masculine realm that he can regain his rightful place in society as future lord of the manor. Susan Sowerby creates a harmonious synergy, drawing two unruly elements into order, for 'Colin walked on one side of her and Mary on the other. Each of them kept looking up at her comfortable, rosy face, secretly curious about the delightful feeling she gave them – a sort of warm, supported feeling. It seemed as if she understood them as Dickon understood his "creatures". She stooped over the flowers and talked about them as if they were children' (276). A metaphorical umbilical cord binds these children to the garden and to Susan, who's described as 'the comfortable, wonderful, mother creature' (251) – she tends both child and garden in a nursery enclosed space, often regarded by critics as an enclosing, nurturing womb, which heightens the mother's significance. For Shirley Foster and Judy Simmons, 'the womb-like seclusion of the garden can be seen as analogous to the power of the mother' (Foster and Simmons 1995: 187), while Mackey observes that the secret garden 'acts as a kind of womb in which the children can be renurtured; it is surely no coincidence that the scene in which Colin meets his father is so redolent of a birth scene' (Mackey 1996: 16).

Another significant mother figure is Colin's dead mother, Lilias Craven, who is an absent presence. Lilias's death provokes her husband, Archibald, to lock up the garden, triggering a psychological, cultural and familial decay. Crucially, the garden belonged to her, and it was where the then-newly married couple spent much of their time, with the underlying hint that perhaps Colin was conceived there. Upon her death or expulsion from the garden, an eternal winter of sterility sets in upon the once fertile space, until it is reawakened by the children (a similar theme is addressed in Oscar Wilde's *The Selfish Giant*). As the garden represents an Edenic space, Lilias's name seems to echo Lilith who, according to Hebrew religion, was the first woman on earth (before Eve). She left the Garden of Eden because of her refusal to be subservient to Adam. Her disappearance from Eden mirrors Lilias's departure: both leave, but their presence is never quite erased and Lilias is very strongly associated with the garden. Could this be the text's feminist undercurrent covertly concealed beneath its surface narrative? Her Fall to her death in the garden triggers Archibald's isolated wandering, as humanity is symbolically excluded from a spoilt Eden. He wanders for ten years (a decade is a common timescale in literature, including the length of time that Odysseus wanders after the Trojan war to get home or the time lapse between Harry Potter's first arrival on the Dursley's doorstep and his induction at Hogwarts).

Susan Sowerby, whose very name suggests the fertile sowing associated with the garden, is juxtaposed with Mrs Lennox, who is portrayed as contravening conventional maternal notions and remaining detached from her daughter, while Colin's absent mother Lilias echoes Lilith. Sandra Gilbert and Susan Gubar refer to this figure from mythology, arguing that Lilith, Adam's first wife, considered herself equal to Adam because she was created not from Adam's rib but, like him, from the dust. As such,

> she objected to lying beneath him, so that when he tried to force her submission, she became enraged and, speaking the Ineffable Name, flew away to the edge of the Red Sea to reside with demons. Threatened by God's angelic emissaries, told that she must return or daily lose a hundred of her demon children to death, Lilith preferred punishment to patriarchal marriage, and she took her revenge against both God and Adam by injuring babies – especially male babies [. . .] the figure of Lilith represents the price women have been told they must pay for attempting to define themselves [. . .] Lilith is locked into a vengeance (child-killing) which can only bring her more suffering (the killing of her own children). (Gilbert and Gubar 1984 [1979]: 35)

Interesting links can be made between Lilias Craven, the sterility of the garden and the debilitated hysterical Colin, who is entombed in a room overlooked by his dead mother's portrait. Lillith is often appropriated by feminist critics as an iconic figure, while Lilias's ghost is apparently haunting the parameters of Burnett's novel. The restoration of patriarchal blood lineage is a vital element of the text's realism, yet undercutting this is the gothic romance of Lilias's death.

Another mother who is arguably an absent presence in the text is Queen Victoria. By 1911, the year of *The Secret Garden*'s publication, Victoria had been dead, significantly, ten years. At this point, Britain still holds a tight imperial grip, but the confidence associated with the Victorian period was beginning to wane: it is only three years later that Britain engages in a World War, partially as an attempt to protect colonial interests in the aftermath of the so-called 'Scramble for Africa'. During Victorian's long reign, England defined itself in Social–Darwinist terms as the purest race and natural leader of subjects. This demise brought with it an insecurity in that image, heightened by the shift from a long reign of increasing prosperity and relative stability ending to a series of short-term successors to the throne. Edward VII reigned from 1901 until his sudden death in 1910, followed by George V, who reigned until 1936 (by comparison Victoria reigned from 1837 to 1901). The nation's populace lost their Mother and the ten-year period might be regarded as a psycho–social wilderness, until the road to the First World War. The ten-year period in the novel is a state of stasis, a kind of eternal winter, in which human contact with the garden and with family members is severed. In keeping with discourses of childhood, the garden as Edenic space is re-entered by the children to bring back the new life of spring and re-growth. During this time, both Colin and Mary have mirrored the garden's sterility in their own halted developmental process. Garden and children are rejuvenated and the barrenness associated with adult culture is reversed, so 'the secret garden was coming alive and two children were coming alive with it' (282). This echoes the Fisher King myth explored in T.S. Eliot's *The Waste Land*, where the impotence of the Fisher King must be cured in order to restore fertility to the barren land (the sterile culture Eliot associated with modernity), just as the Secret Garden exists in a state of limbo until its re-discovery. Humphrey Carpenter writes, 'is not the garden, dead and overgrown when Mary first finds it, reminiscent of another ancient symbol, the Waste Land? Its dead state seems profoundly related to the sickness of Colin, who is a kind of wounded Fisher King' (Carpenter 1985: 189). The garden, though, is dormant rather than dead, for it 'isn't a quite dead garden' (81). Colin is not necessarily emblematic of the Fisher King, for his sickness is symptomatic of the sterile brokenness of his father.

Being a walled garden which encloses the children within it also corresponds to Froebel's recommendations, for 'Here the gardens and respective beds of the children must be surrounded by the garden of the whole [. . .] The part for the general is the inclosing, as it were, the protecting part; that for the children, the inclosed, protected part' (Froebel 1899: 219–20). To reach the inner secret garden, Mary must pass through a labyrinthian structure of outer 'protecting' gardens, for 'she liked [. . .] the feeling that when its beautiful old walls shut her in, no one knew where she was. It seemed almost like being shut out of the world in some fairy place' (89). The walls of the garden serve as a border to protect a spatial paradise from outside interference. Are those borders, however, permeable or even imprisoning? After all, the novel tells us that Mary is 'shut in' by 'old walls' – simultaneously conjuring a sense of nurturing and incarcerating. This Edenic threshold is breached through the mingling of social class: Dickon is working-class, albeit in a rustically pure format. He is strongly associated with nature in the text and has parallels with the mythical figure of Pan. Mary first encounters him 'Sitting under a tree, with his back against it, playing on a rough wooden pipe' (96), and he is surrounded by animals, presented as a kind of nature god, who is at one with his environment – such aspects could offer an ecocritical reading of the novel, where the significance of the balance of nature is paramount. His mystical qualities are emphasized throughout the book, for 'it seemed as if he might be a sort of wood fairy' (110); 'his fox and his crow and his squirrels and his lamb [. . .] seemed almost to be a part of himself' (201). Mary and Colin want to learn Dickon's Yorkshire dialect, which could be read as a way of "controlling" his lower class status. His dialect is 'like a native dialect in India. Very clever people try to learn them' (194). An association is clearly made between a native in India and Dickon as a native of Yorkshire. Phillips argues that 'the colonizer learned the language not to "please" the colonized but to cement his own social control' (Phillips 1993: 185). Notably, Rousseau recommends that the language of rustic peasants is learned by children sent to the country in a way which clearly reinforces power structures.

Along with his Mother, Dickon plays a significant role in healing Mary, Colin and their garden, and his lamb is associated with their sickness: 'The new-born lamb Dickon had found [. . .] lying by its dead mother' (198). The orphaned lamb that has lost its mother echoes the orphaned children – all of whom Dickon nurtures with milk. The lamb also serves as a Christian motif within this Edenic space, symbolizing the lamb of God and reinforcing connotations of innocence. But Dickon also symbolizes erotic pagan myths as well as Christian myths. In Greek mythology the figure of Pan is highly sexual, for

> there was something of the beast about him [. . .] Pan was ithy-phallic, lascivious and debauched [. . .] He was constantly pur-suing nymphs [. . .] Caves rang out with the cries which escaped from their lips in the course of some furtive coupling with the god. However, Pan was no less interested in boys who often satis-fied his needs [. . .] He was the god of the inexplicable. (Comte 1994 [1988]: 156–7)

Like Colin's queer state, Pan cannot be straightforwardly explained, while music from Pan's pipes 'induced mating' (Comte 1994 [1988]: 156). When Mary first encounters Dickon, he is playing his phal-lically symbolic pipe in the woods in spring, the mating season, while in the secret garden the robin is nest building. The garden shifts from Edenic innocence to fertile erotic space, so complicat-ing its signification. References to 'blood' and coming 'alive' could refer to sexual awakening, the cycle of nature: death, rebirth and the shift from winter to spring. Dickon is first encountered in the woods – these border the enclosed secret garden and suggest a wild Otherness emanating from the lower class on its hinterlands, which is never far away from impinging upon the artificial control of the garden's idealized Edenic space. Dickon, the potentially erotic figure, also feeds Mary and Colin, as well as nourishing the gar-den and its creatures. In children's literature, the act of eating and drinking is often associated with Freud's theories of childhood sexuality and the oral phase. Throughout Burnett's story, the chil-dren gorge themselves in abundant pleasure, partaking in 'a regular feast' (277). Rousseau recommends,

> The most natural tastes ought also to be the simplest [. . .] Our first food is milk [. . .] Let us preserve in the child his primary taste as much as possible. Let his nourishment be common and simple [. . .] to gratify children's appetites, there is no need to arouse their sensuality but only a need to satisfy it [. . .] Fruit, dairy products, some baked thing [. . .] for meat is not natural to man [. . .] It is, above all, important not to denature this primitive taste and make children carnivorous. (Rousseau 1991 [1762]: 151–3)

Rousseau clearly links childhood orality with sexuality and its plenitude in the novel suggests eroticism and fecundity.

The garden can be seen as a space where gender and class barriers are temporarily dissolved, as three children unite in their common childhood love of nature. Mary, remember, is unwanted by her biological mother, who 'had not wanted a little girl at all' (1). In a sense, then, she is the girl who should have been a boy and, in her failure to live up to such an expectation, she is discarded and then orphaned. Many critics have argued that Colin is Mary's alter ego, suggesting that her lack as female can only be culturally compensated with phallic displacement and association – she is finally overshadowed by the boy she never is. From the moment Colin enters the garden, Mary is dislocated from it: while she re-discovered and tended it, Colin lays claim to it through his social authority as next in line to the Craven estate. He says to Ben Weatherstaff, 'I'm your master [. . .] when my father is away. And you are to obey me. This is my garden' (226) and he reminds Mary, 'It is my garden now' (230). The realism in the novel is constantly undercut by a romantic discourse, with influences from Gothic romance (Archibald is seemingly a hunchback living in a Gothic mansion), and fairy tales, for instance. The realism appears, like the garden, on the surface. But when you dig beneath that topsoil, what lies beneath is a more romantic mode, often associated with a feminine resistance to patriarchal masculine forms of writing, such as the feminist potential lurking in the text through Lilias. Gothically, Colin is associated with the wolf in the *Little Red Riding Hood* fairy story. When Mary first encounters him, like, the wolf, he is in bed: 'His grey eyes opening so wide that they seemed immense [. . .] He stared and stared and stared. Mary could not help noticing what strange eyes he had. They were agate-grey and they looked too big for his face' (125). Mary says to him 'What big eyes you've got' (209), while he even describes himself as 'a boy animal' (154) and, 'I screamed out loud and bit her hand' (153) – he has wolfish traits. Interestingly, Lilith gave birth to demon-children and Lilias dies not long after Colin's (who is 'queer' and animal-like) birth. It is no surprise that such a wolfish character ousts Mary from her garden and lays claim to the Craven estate through his inherited bloodline. Though Mary and Dickon unearth the garden, her gender role and his class role are subordinated and replaced by the new master of the manor: focalized through the servants' eyes on the final page, we observe a rejuvenated 'Master Colin!' (298) walking steadily by his father's side. Notice the shift from Mother in the so-called feminine nurturing space of the Garden to Father as Colin gets ready to assume his rightful position in society. By leading Archibald Craven back to the garden, the Father's paradise lost is regained, but the son is also positioning himself within his patriarchal legacy. Several critics have debated whether or not this ending renders the text conservative with the status quo maintained rather than challenged, so that its conclusion foregrounds 'the conservatism which has also been implicit in its portrayal of class relations' (Foster and Simmons 1995: 189). As Mary is replaced by Colin as the locus of attention at the end of the novel, so, too, is the working-class Dickon's crucial role in the healing process swept aside 'in the finale's emphasis on reconciliation between father and son' (Foster and Simmons 1995: 189). It also serves to frame the childhood liberation from parental figures by the 'removal and the return of parents' (Foster and Simmons 1995: 189). Crucially, they argue that social class and gender divisions are reinforced by a return to the status quo which further excludes 'Mary and Dickon from the centre of love as well as from power' (Foster and Simmons 1995: 189). Heather Murray, alternatively, questions whether this female-authored text's seeming validation of the status quo through the systematic erasure of Mary and Dickon is not actually 'descriptive rather than prescriptive, telling us the way of the world rather than how it ought to be?' (Murray 1985: 40–1). Other critics have countered the privileging of the ending, arguing that everything else that happens in the text is of equal validity rather than just one final page, and that the reader's recollection of the story tends to reinstate Mary through her significance in memory as an integral part of the book. The complexities of Burnett's novel and its Gothic undercurrents imply that any attempt to simplify its meaning will be overturned: like the multiple layers of soil in the garden, unearthing her text critically reveals the richness of interpretative possibilities.

C.S. LEWIS – *THE LION, THE WITCH AND THE WARDROBE* (1950)

Lewis's *The Lion, the Witch and the Wardrobe* (1950) charts the adventure of the four evacuated Pevensie children (Lucy, Susan, Peter and Edmund) during the Second World War, who 'were sent away from London during the war because of the air-raids' (Lewis 1980 [1950]: 9). It is the first instalment in the *Chronicles of Narnia*. Though choosing the medium of fantasy, Lewis is influenced by social events, since many children faced evacuation to rural environments during the war. Themes of home are raised, as the children are evicted from their familial home and relocated to an unfamiliar space, inevitably leading to separation anxiety and a journey that helps to heal the lack of security felt in their uncanny environment. Initially, the journey from an urban to a rural landscape transports them from London to rural England, which typifies the influence of Victorian thinking concerning childhood and nature. It also signals a return to a womb-like security, away from the horrors of war to re-emerge changed but unharmed from social trauma and ready to return home. The war raging in the world that the children have escaped from is then mirrored in Narnia, where they are safe to explore the trauma of conflict within the parameters of a framed fantasy world. Narnia is the secondary world that exists beyond the wardrobe's back, framing a primary world that they can return to. As Naomi Wood argues, 'This degree of control does offer a degree of security' for 'under the narrator's guiding hand, only so much can go wrong in Narnia' (Montgomery and Watson 2009: 270). While 'the child protagonists may temporarily suffer discomfort, hunger, and fear, no doubt arises that the Narrator and his image, Aslan, are in control' (Montgomery and Watson 2009: 270). Time also functions as a safety device because, while time passes in Narnia, it is frozen on this side of the wardrobe. In Narnia, the children are empowered by overcoming dangerous adventures and reach adulthood, for, 'These two Kings and two Queens governed Narnia well, and long and happy was their reign' (166), yet when they return to their old world towards the end of the narrative, 'It was the same day and the same hour of the day on which they had all gone into the wardrobe to hide' (170), allowing them to return safely to their childhood. In keeping with much children's fiction, the Penvensie children are part of a prophesy for, 'We get the impression that Narnia has been waiting for the[m]' (Grenby 2008: 159).

Upon arrival at the Professor's, they learn that the house is a labyrinthine structure of hidden 'stairs and passages' (10) and its wild rural location exists on the peripheries of their recognized urban civilization, for there are 'mountains' and 'woods' (10). Temporarily placed on the Other side of familiarity, the untamed landscape serves as a trope for the imagination, a space beyond adult control that they can wander through, for, 'That old chap will let us do anything we like' (9). Following the conventions of children's literature, the children are liberated from parental authority so that they can find new worlds and explore uninhibited, but with the reassurance that the primary world is always waiting on this side of the wardrobe door. Another indicator of the imaginative realm being housed in the Professor's Gothic home is 'a whole series of rooms that led into each other' that 'were lined with books' (11). Having walls lined with books, undoubtedly including fictional reads, this mysterious house – 'which even [the Professor] knew so little about' (50) – is steeped in the imagination and serves as a space through which the children can explore their unconscious anxieties and desires. Like the mirror passed through in *Alice*, the wardrobe 'has a looking-glass in the door', emphasizing that Narnia is a realm on the Other side of the mirror. On this side of the mirror, the conventions of the 'real' world are framed and reflected back at us but, behind that glass lies Narnia, which will comment from a different angle on events in our world using fantasy's distortive lens. The use of binaries emphasizes the function of the mirror as a fantasy device to explore a different perspective for, while '[i]t is summer there' in Lucy's familiar realm, 'it is winter in Narnia' (17). In Lewis's commentary upon the horrors of the Second World War, the innocent connotations of summer associated with Lucy's childhood are abruptly inverted to symbolize winter as experience with its sterile, dead and cold world that lacks freedom and happiness. Like the trauma of war in Lucy's adult world, Narnia is blighted by an unnaturally eternal winter, rather like the Fisher King myth used by T.S. Eliot in *The Waste Land* to consider the horrors of the First World War. Another intertextual echo of *Alice* occurs when 'Lucy found herself walking through the wood arm in arm' (17–19) with Mr Tumnus the Faun, which is reminiscent of Alice walking with her arm round the Fawn's neck in the wood in *Through the Looking-Glass*.

Narnia is often read by critics as a Christian allegory, with Aslan the Lion representing Christ. The very mention of his name invokes 'that strange feeling' in the children, 'like the first signs of spring, like good news' (74). He spreads Christian good news, saving and liberating Narnia's inhabitants from the tyranny of its usurper Queen, the White Witch. His return to Narnia thaws the land from its eternal winter with the onslaught of spring and its connotations of rebirth and fertility overcoming sterility and death. While they learn that 'she has made a magic so that it is always winter in Narnia – always winter, but it never gets to Christmas' (42), this is overcome as 'it grew foggier and warmer' (107) until '[s]hafts of delicious sunlight struck down on to the forest floor' (110) and 'the whole wood was ringing with birds' music' (111), for, 'This is *Spring* [. . .] Your winter has been destroyed, I tell you! This is Aslan's doing' (112). Even his first arrival alters the balance of power in Narnia because 'Father Christmas' (99) appears, saying, 'She has kept me out for a long time, but I have got in at last. Aslan is on the move. The Witch's magic is weakening' (99). Order is restored through his intervention, while he sacrifices his life to save Edmund who would otherwise be punished for his betrayal, just as Christ died atoning for humanity's sins, according to Christian discourse. In keeping with Christ's crucifixion, Aslan, too, is tied up and 'the whole crowd of creatures' were 'kicking him, hitting him, spitting on him, jeering at him' (140). Killed by the White Witch's knife on the sacrificial Stone Table, his resurrection mirrors Christ's, for 'shining in the sunrise, larger than they had seen him before, shaking his mane [. . .] stood Aslan himself' (147). Aslan dies and is reborn at Easter, serving as an allegory for the Christian belief in death and rebirth portrayed in Christ's Easter Ascension.

Lewis draws upon Christian mythology in his use of fantasy as a way of dealing with psychosocial ruptures in society, and uses the imaginative space of Narnia to pedagogically reflect upon Christian notions of good and evil. The restoration of order involves a reinforcement of patriarchal values, particularly in relation to gender roles. The White Witch, epitomized as evil, wields her wand as a phallic symbol of her usurping power while the true King, Aslan is absent. Notably, when she is defeated, Edmund who had been hitherto tantalized and then victimized by her, breaks her wand with his phallic symbol, bringing 'his sword smashing down on her wand' (162) and symbolizing a restoration of his masculine power over her and returning Narnia to patriarchal order. The White Witch represents the monstrous feminine, which patriarchy must keep in check: 'she's no Daughter of Eve' but is from 'your father Adam's first wife, her they called Lilith. And she was one of the Jinn' (76). This echoes the discussion earlier of Lilith in *The Secret Garden*, with her demonic power being feared and controlled by masculine authority. As such, she is dehumanized in Lewis's story, a descendant of she who refused to be subservient to male authority. As a Christian allegory, Lewis's text punishes her fully for defying patriarchy and for the alleged crimes of her Mother, for 'the figure of Lilith represents the price women have been told they must pay for attempting to define themselves' (Gilbert and Gubar 1984 [1979]: 35). The White Witch is unmaternal, suggesting a sterility as cold as her landscape, and women without so-called maternal instincts are considered unnatural even now in society. Rather than child rearing, her association with Lilith equates her with infanticide: on the other side of the mirrored wardrobe, ambitious women are punished as demonic in a Christian affirmation of patriarchy. Edmund is initially lured through the consumption of enchanted Turkish Delight, suggesting an exotic Eastern Otherness that is endangering the security of this British child. Having consumed her wares, Edmund is ravenous for more, for it 'was enchanted Turkish Delight' and 'anyone who tasted it would want more and more of it, and would even, if they were allowed, go on eating it till they killed themselves' (38). This moment echoes the temptation of Adam by Eve after her consumption of the apple and also intertextualizes Christina Rossetti's 'Goblin Market' (1862), where Laura devours forbidden fruits from Goblin men and almost dies until she is redeemed by her sister Lizzie's sacrifice.

Those regarded as good are those who follow unquestioningly conservative traditions, such as obedience and gender dichotomies. So, the 'old she-beaver' sits 'in the corner with a thread in her mouth working busily at her sewing machine' (68), engaged in an acceptable female domestic chore, while Mr Beaver 'went out of the house (Peter went with him)' to catch fish (69), indicating a clear division of labour based on domestic tasks for females and outdoor pursuits for males. While Peter is off learning to hunt, 'the girls were helping Mrs Beaver to fill the kettle and lay the table and cut the bread and put the plates in the oven and draw a huge jug of beer for Mr Beaver' (69). This male dominance is further asserted through language use, for 'everyone took as much as he wanted to go with his potatoes' (70). Despite female presence, 'everyone' is reduced to masculine pronouns, until the narrator attempts to accommodate others: 'when each person had got his (or her) cup of tea' (72). Partitioning off females with parenthesis, however, only further indicates that their value is secondary as an add-on to the dominant male authority. The feminist theorist Dale Spender similarly argues that such masculine linguistic dominance 'is a move towards the concept that male is the universal category, that male is the norm' (Burke et al. 2000: 150). This dominant privileging of one sex over the other with 'the use of *man* and *he* as terms to denote a male, but on occasion to encompass a female' clearly indicates 'an example of a sexist linguistic structure' (Burke et al. 2000: 148). Lewis defines normality as Christian goodness and anything other to this is regarded as mistaken if not downright evil, for 'the good tends to align with heterosexuality, with sexual division of labor and society', while '[p]erversity, often shading into evil, is good pursued through faulty humanism: progressive, socialist, and feminist efforts to institute programmatic social change' (Montgomery and Watson 2009: 270). In Lewis's series, 'to obey Aslan is simply to align oneself with good' (Montgomery and Watson 2009: 270). After the inverted misrule of the White Witch, a conservative status quo is resumed in the climactic battle of good versus evil towards the end of the novel, mirroring the war beyond the world of the wardrobe. Evil is feminized and goodness is embodied in the Christian battle which deliberately excludes female participation, for 'battles are ugly when women fight' (101). As with traditional wars, women are expected to work in supportive ancillary roles like nursing: Lucy is given a bottle of healing potion to administer to the wounded.

J.K. ROWLING – *HARRY POTTER* (1997–2007)

For Rosemary Jackson, 'fantastic literature points to or suggests the basis upon which cultural order rests', momentarily inviting the 'illegality' of 'that which lies outside the law, that which is outside dominant value systems' (Jackson 1998 [1981]: 4) to be present. The *Harry Potter* series, as fantasy, corresponds to Jackson's interpretation: it too engages with that which society renders silent or invisible. Fantasy allows a writer to comment upon society through the use of metaphor and symbolism rather than directly, as we would expect in a realist text. For Armitt, 'the fantastic' is 'a form of writing which is about opening up subversive spaces' (Armitt 1996: 3), while Gooderham points out that '[f]antasy is a metaphorical mode' that approaches reality through an alternative narrative lens to realism to say something differently (Gooderham 1995: 173). So, the questions we might ask are, to what extent is the *Harry Potter* series 'opening up subversive spaces' and where, or what 'human concerns' is it addressing in 'a metaphorical mode'? We might also consider the combination of fantasy and children's fiction – is it more subversive when fantasy is addressed to a child reader? It is important to recognize where the fantasy realm in *Harry Potter* is: it is not located in a different world, but in the interstices of the recognizable and familiar. Hence, it is in Diagon Alley – or diagonally. The space where Harry boards the Hogwarts Express exists within King's Cross Station – Platform 9 and 3/4 is a fantasy space located within the familiarity of platforms 9 and 10. Spatially, this other world exists Diagon Alley to the realist dimension of everyday London and its familiar suburbs, but remains largely undiscovered by this realm, though the boundaries do blur as the series progresses. Likewise, for Julia Kristeva, the semiotic exists underneath the symbolic order, yet erupts into it periodically, while travel can occur between both worlds as Harry, Ron and Hermione escape from the Death Eaters to London's Tottenham Court Road in *Deathly Hallows*.

So what issues might the *Harry Potter* novels be addressing? Rowling herself is an interesting starting point. Much of the biographical information about Rowling has become as fairy tale-like as her novels, in the sense of a rags-to-riches story of a single mother on the dole becoming extraordinarily wealthy (of course, such stories fail to point out that she was born into a relatively middle-class family, had a university education and taught English abroad). However, her status at the time as a single mother (she has since married) who became very successful was a strong challenge to the then Conservative Government of Prime Minister John Major. In 1993, he blamed single-parent families 'for the breakdown in discipline among the nation's children' (Smith 2001: 118), a declaration that stigmatized Rowling (herself a single parent claiming state benefits at the time). Notably, upon gaining celebrity author status in later years, she became ambassador for the National Council for One-Parent Families and made a strong speech against the then-shadow Home Secretary for defining the conventional nuclear family as "the norm". Alluding to the fact that 'a quarter of Britain's children are being brought up by single parents', Rowling asserted:

> Ann Widdecombe, justifying her remarks against lone parents [. . .] feels society should have a 'preferred norm'. We may not be

some people's preferred norm but we are here. We should judge how civilized a society is not by what it prefers to call normal but by how it treats its most vulnerable members. When you take poverty out of the question, the vast majority from one-parent families do just as well as children from couple families. (Smith 2001: 196)

Since gaining status as a celebrity author, Rowling has made use of her voice in order to champion social causes. This idea of normality is something which runs through all of the *Harry Potter* novels: even Harry himself as the hero of these books is perceived in the hyper-normal sheltered world of the Dursleys as something of a freak. *The Philosopher's Stone* invites us into the novel through a discussion of normality and marginalized positions within that centralized norm. The opening sentence notes that 'Mr and Mrs Dursley of number four, Privet Drive, were proud to say that they were perfectly normal, thank you very much' (7), while 'The Dursleys often spoke about Harry [. . .] as though he wasn't there – or rather, as though he was something very nasty that couldn't understand them, like a slug' (22). Like those marginalized from mainstream normative society, Harry symbolizes this silencing and rendering invisible the Other – he is housed, not in the central parameters of the family home (the nuclear family was argued to be the very backbone of British values and society according to John Major), but at its fringes. Ideas of homelessness and the quest for a sense of self as well as home crop up time and again in children's literature. He resides in the cupboard under the stairs, sharing it with spiders. His existence does not allow him to belong to the Dursley's version of normality, which is a satirical stab at dominant social positions. It is no accident that when he comes out of the closet (an intended pun, given the fact that Harry is queer insofar as he is against the norm imposed by the Dursleys, and represents Otherness in their world), that it is to embrace his new self as a wizard, much to the horror of the Dursley's, who 'swore when we took him in we'd put a stop to that rubbish [. . .] swore we'd stamp it out of him!' (43). By 'stamping *it* out of him' we can only assume that he has been subjected to a kind of aversion therapy tactic. It is only in the fantasy realm beyond the claustrophobic framing device of Privet Drive's so-called real world that Harry can develop his full potential. In that sense it is a fantasy *Bildungsroman*, which charts his journey from a mistreated, demonized Other, who has been misinformed about his own parental origins and heritage, towards the fulfilment of his education and self-knowledge.

Interestingly, the revered normality of the Dursley household is portrayed as having a very superficial veneer – underneath it lurks a grotesquely dysfunctional family centred on Dudley as a tantrum-ridden, self-indulged, obese child and any secrets are thoroughly repressed, such as Harry, who is rendered invisible to them. No engagement with other possibilities from the mindset of this suffocating authoritarian surrogate father figure is offered: *'Don't ask questions* – that was the first rule for a quiet life in the Dursleys' (20). Also repressed in this ideal family haven is creativity itself, where any inkling of the imagination is utterly quashed, for Vernon Dursley 'didn't approve of imagination' (10). When Harry talks about his dream of a flying motorbike (which is an earlier childhood memory of his delivery to the Dursley's doorstep by Hagrid), Uncle Vernon 'nearly crashed the car' (24) through his over-reaction because, 'If there was one thing the Dursleys hated even more than asking questions, it was his talking about anything acting in a way it shouldn't, no matter if it was in a dream or even a cartoon – they seemed to think he might get dangerous ideas' (24). In psychoanalytic terms, Vernon Dursley is a patriarch within the Symbolic Order. Harry escapes from this to the imaginary, semi-otic, so-called feminine realm of fantasy. Vernon is the director of a drill company – he drills the normality of the symbolic order into his household. He is a castrating Oedipal father figure for Harry – pertaining to Jacques Lacan's Law of the Phallus. In many ways, then, the use of magic in the novel, and Harry's realization that he is a wizard, works metaphorically to consider the importance of the imagination and creativity, things crucial to Rowling herself as a writer. Without such traits, the implication is that everyone would fall into the unthinking, unchallenging, uniformity of life at number 4 Privet Drive (this is very similar to ideas espoused in Philip Pullman's *Northern Lights* when he argues that without free-dom to challenge mindsets and to generate ideas through creativity, then the universes and their inhabitants will become nothing more than mindless robotic automatons).

The series further charts the shift from primary to second-ary world through the spatial description of landscape. Harry's journey to Hogwarts is marked by distinctive changes to the regimental suburbia of Privet Drive, with its carefully tended lawns and hedges. The normative world of the Dursleys is very static in its claustrophobic incarceration of Harry, while his journey of self-knowledge involves motion, boarding the train, that moves him towards his more loving home of Hogwarts. So '[t]he countryside now flying past the window was becoming wilder. The neat fields had gone. Now there were woods, twisting rivers and dark green hills' (78). The carefully domesticized control of nature in civilized middle-England is left behind in the move towards a much wilder, untamed, Gothic landscape. The Dursleys' representation of the Self of normative society view Harry as the marginalized freak or Other and, it is therefore, expected that he will move towards an environment that reflects his socially marginalized position; thus his wizard world is located on the hinterlands of civilized norms. The suggestion is also that the Hogwarts Express is carrying Harry to a northern landscape, which is more rugged and mountainous – he journeys North to the colder climes of a wilder Scottish hinterland with a Gothic landscape, with all the social and political implications which that raises in relation to cultural norms of self and Other. Rowling reflects that

> My parents [. . .] met on a train heading north to Scotland from King's Cross Station in London [. . .] Hogwarts School of Witchcraft and Wizardry was the first thing I concentrated on [. . .] Logically it had to be set in a secluded place, and pretty soon I settled on Scotland in my mind. I think it was in subconscious tribute to where my parents had married. (Fraser 2002 [2000]: 23)

For Margaret Elphinstone, 'the location of the fantastic in the real world is often tied in with a precise topography of the Scottish landscape' (www.arts.gla.ac.uk/scotlit/asls/MElphinstone.html).

Though Dursleyian normative society cast Harry in the role of abnormal, as a hero he is, in fact, extremely ordinary. Aunt Petunia carries out a character assassination on Harry's parents, saying of her sister Lily, 'I was the only one who saw her for what she was – a freak! [. . .] Then she met that Potter at school and they left and got married and had you, and of course I knew you'd be just the same, just as strange, just as – as – *abnormal*' (44). In order to draw in the child reader so that he/she identifies with the hero, however,

Harry is painted in very ordinary terms. His status as outsider and abnormal can apply to any number of possible cultural issues in which an individual might feel alienated. The name Potter suggests that which can be moulded or shaped or can mould (conveying the notion of childhood malleability). Meanwhile, 'The ordinariness of Harry is magnificently emphasized by his name, which clearly stands out as plain and unpretentious beside Dumbledore, McGonagall, or Draco Malfoy', for 'Harry's name underscores his "everyman" nature, signaling to the readers: "He is just like one of you"' (Nikolajeva, in Heilman 2003: 131). This is important for the child reader to identify with the hero in children's literature. Even Harry's physical description is unremarkable, for

> Perhaps it had something to do with living in a dark cupboard, but Harry had always been small and skinny for his age [. . .] Harry had a thin face, knobbly knees [. . .] He wore round glasses held together with a lot of Sellotape because of all the times Dudley had punched him on the nose. (20)

He is no Adonis-like figure; instead just an ordinary boy. But, what marks him out is his extraordinary powers which are symbolized by a visible sign: 'The only thing Harry liked about his appearance was a very thin scar on his forehead which was shaped like a bolt of lighting' (20). The scar literally marks him out for higher things, setting him apart from the common herd; it is simultaneously a sign of his great power and also great loss, a bit like a stigmata for the entire world to see. It is not only from the Muggle world that he is marked out as being different; even in his own wizard domain he is perceived to be special. Professor McGonagall says, 'These people will never understand him! He'll be famous – a legend – I wouldn't be surprised if today was known as Harry Potter Day in future – there will be books written about Harry – every child in our world will know his name!' (15). McGonagall's remark is strangely prophetic because art reflects life given the phenomenal Pottermania that appears to have swept across the globe. The momentous success of the novels has had a knock-on effect to their author, for

> The burst of publicity terrified me [. . .] I felt frozen by all the attention [. . .] there are other more disconcerting sides to that level of publicity – having your photograph appear regularly in

the paper is not something I ever anticipated [. . .] There are times – and I don't want to sound ungrateful – when I would gladly give back some of the money in exchange for time and peace to write [. . .] I've become famous, and I'm not very comfortable with that. Because of the fame some really difficult things have happened, and it's required a great effort of will to shut them out. (Fraser 2002 [2000]: 30–9)

Hitting back at such attention spawned the creation of the unscrupulous *Daily Prophet* journalist Reeta Skeeter in *Goblet of Fire* who continually makes up stories about Harry.

McGonagall's reference to Harry's fame occurs in the first chapter, entitled 'The Boy Who Lived' and such signification results in Harry being presented as something of a messiah figure – his arrival and survival against the odds by defeating Voldemort's Satan-like evil forces ensures that the Wizard world and, by implication, the Muggle world, are safer, freer places. His defeat of Voldemort allows his Wizard community the first opportunity in 'eleven years' (13) to celebrate and indulge themselves in feasting. Hagrid fills in some of the blanks in Harry's history when he says, 'No one ever lived after he decided ter kill 'em, no one except you' (45), for 'somethin' about you finished him, Harry. There was somethin' goin' on that night he hadn't counted on – *I* dunno what it was, no one does – but somethin' about you stumped him, all right' (47). Like Lyra in Pullman's *His Dark Materials*, Harry is a chosen saviour child, although Pullman's representation of good and evil are far more complex than Rowling's in many ways. Nikolajeva argues that *His Dark Materials* 'portrays characters with dubious moral qualities, including the young protagonists' since Lyra 'is not as pure and innocent as traditional fantasy prescribes' (Nikolajeva, in Heilman 2003: 136). Further, 'Lyra, like Eve in the Bible, will be subject to a temptation. It is, however, far from clear whether she is supposed to fall or withstand, and in the first place what consequences either of these actions will have. With Harry, on the other hand, we can be more or less sure that his task is to fight Voldemort, not to assist him' (Nikolajeva, in Heilman 2003: 136).

Nikolajeva's statement is problematic because Harry and Voldemort's identities are blurred – they are doppelgangers in many ways. But what seems to give Harry power over Voldemort is his position as innocent child – he is only one year old when his parents are killed. Harry initially defeats Voldemort without any action on his part, so the overwhelming suggestion is that it is Harry's status of purity that leads to the victory, reflecting a tradition in children's literature that reaches back to the associations made between childhood purity and Romantic discourse. For Nikolajeva, 'The premise for the romantic child hero is the idealization of childhood that developed during the Romantic era. It is based on the belief in the child as innocent and, therefore, capable of conquering evil' (Nikolajeva, in Heilman 2003: 128). In keeping with this Romanticism, 'Harry is no exception. His chief strength is the very fact that he is a child, and it is stressed that already, as an infant, he had the power to protect himself against Voldemort. His intrinsic goodness is his most momentous weapon' (Nikolajeva, in Heilman 2003: 128). That argument is problematic because part of Harry's journey is that he, like Pullman's Lyra, is moving ever-closer to the experience of adolescence, a fact about which Rowling is all too aware, and she very much echoes Pullman in her support for children's literature to be allowed to reach this level of maturity for its characters. In a *Newsnight* interview by Jeremy Paxman on 19 June 2003, prior to the release of *Order of the Phoenix*, Paxman asks Rowling, 'Harry and Ron and Hermione are all going to be older. How are they going to change?'. To which Rowling responds, 'Quite a lot because I find it quite sinister, the way that, looking back at the *Famous Five* books for example, I think 21 adventures or 20 or something, they never had a hormonal impulse'. Paxman says, 'But that's the usual pattern of children's books isn't it? *Swallows and Amazons* is the same isn't it? The children never age'. Rowling responds,

And it reaches its apotheosis in Peter Pan obviously, where it is quite explicit, and I find that very sinister. I had a very forthright letter from a woman who had heard me say that Harry is going to have his first date or something and she said, 'Please don't do that, that's awful. I want these books to be a world where my children can escape to'. She literally said 'free from hurt and fear', and I'm thinking 'Have you read the books? What are talking about free from hurt and fear? Harry goes through absolute hell every time he returns to school'. So I think a bit of snogging would alleviate matters. (www.newsvote.bbc.co.uk/mpapps/pagetools/print/news.bbc.co.uk/1/hi/entertainment/)

Despite his unathletic build, Harry is nevertheless a sporting hero in the Wizard game of Quidditch and is, symbolically, the team's seeker. Though an ordinary name, Harry is also a royal name (Prince Harry is heir to the throne); and it has associations with Shakespeare's Henry IV, for example. As seeker, his keen eye for hunting down the Golden Snitch relates to the fact that Harry wears glasses for short-sightedness, suggesting an internal-looking journey of progression towards self-discovery rather than merely looking outwards. This idea of inner sight and seeking is further evident in the influence of the detective story genre in the *Harry Potter* novels because, in many ways, they follow the traditional who-dunnit of pursuing clues and seeking out answers to riddles (of course, the ultimate riddle to solve is Tom Riddle). The novels have been compared to the James Bond stories, where we know that the hero will prevail and win the day, but nevertheless we get caught up in the unfolding of the action. As clues are followed in each novel, where the trail inevitably leads to Lord Voldemort (an anagram of his real name, Tom Marvolo Riddle), Harry, in turn, comes ever closer to finding out more about the role that Voldemort has played and continues to play in his own story. In that sense, the Gothic castle of Hogwarts school symbolizes the troubled psyche of Harry, with its numerous dungeons, subterranean passages and secret entrances, in the depths of which he often plunges in order to move another step closer to his adversary. Because of this detective story plot device, there is a repetitive structure to each of the novels, which follow a broadly similar journey from Privet Drive to Hogwarts and back again, with all of the danger and mystery solving occurring in between. In order to advance the stories, though, there must be progression as well as repetition, so each story unveils some new information. As Harry gets older, the parameters of his world expand beyond merely Hogwarts and Privet Drive: for instance, he is allowed to venture into the village of Hogsmeade as an older student, or he goes to the Quidditch World Cup, and, by the final book, *Deathly Hallows* (2007), he and his companions cover large areas of the country while hiding from the Death Eaters.

A crucial issue in the novels is 'Blood', which has ties to ideas of normality and abnormality mentioned earlier. While Harry does manage to escape the harsh treatment and labelling meted out to him at the hands of the Dursleys as he embraces his new-found homeland of the Wizard world, nevertheless it, too, has its divisive hierarchical systems. Draco Malfoy is the character in the first novel associated with this issue of preserving the blood lineage of wizard generations. On his first encounter with Harry, his obsession with this emerges as he asks Harry whether his parents were '*our* kind' (61), referring to pure-blood wizards. He explains that, 'I really don't think they should let the other sort in, do you? They're just not the same, they've never been brought up to know our ways. Some of them have never even heard of Hogwarts until they get the letter, imagine. I think they should keep it in the old wizarding families' (61). Ironically, Harry himself had never heard of Hogwarts until receiving his letter and his mother is a Muggle, so he does not adhere to Malfoy's depiction of a pure-blood wizard race. This culminates in *Chamber of Secrets* in Malfoy's hostile prejudice against Hermoine, whose parents are both Muggles, referring to her as 'a filthy little Mudblood' (86). The blood motif, then, has emerged fully at this point, as Ron explains to Harry, 'Mudblood's a really foul name for someone who was muggle-born – you know, non-magic parents. There are some wizards – like Malfoy's family – who think they're better than everyone else because they're what people call pure-blood' (89). Draco's name sounds like Dracula, as he vampirically preys on the significance of other's blood while, interestingly, as dentists, Hermione's parents focus on teeth. Draco is not the creator of this prejudice, he is merely a supporter and instigator of it, for Ron explains that it is a clearly established cultural prejudice, like those in our own society. Malfoy's prejudice extends to other marginalized groups. His view of Hagrid is that 'he's a sort of *savage*' (60) – Hagrid is half giant and half wizard, and the view of such marginalized cultures is explored further in the later books like *Goblet of Fire*. Malfoy also opposes pure-blood wizards on social class terms, constantly berating Roy Weasley because of his family's relative poverty – he warns Harry, 'You'll soon find out some wizarding families are much better than others, Potter. You don't want to go making friends with the wrong sort' (81). Neville Longbottom is another of Malfoy's victims insofar as he is not perceived to be as elite in intelligence as a wizard ought to be. He singles out Gryffindor as the school house which houses all of those less able groupings, explaining, 'You know how I think they choose people for the Gryffindor team [. . .] It's people they feel sorry for. See, there's Potter, who's got no parents, then there's the Weasleys, who've got no money – you should be on the team, Longbottom, you've got no brains' (163).

Suman Gupta writes, 'In *Stone* the connection between Malfoy and his family and Voldemort and the Dark Side is left unclear [. . .] It is one of several kinds of evil – like the brutality of the Dursleys and the fear that Voldemort inspires', while 'In *Chamber* there is a sudden convergence between the presentation of Malfoy (and his family connections) and Voldemort (the Dark Side), and it has to do with prejudice against Muggle blood' (Gupta 2003: 100). Thus, the Malfoy family and Voldemort unite within 'the Dark Side' through 'a certain ideological perspective, an explicitly fascist ideology that wishes to preserve the purity of Magic blood from any taint of Muggle blood' (Gupta 2003: 100–1.) This 'theme of blood as lineage, analogous to race in our world, simmers away without being emphasized in *Prisoner* [. . .] but comes back squarely to the centre in *Goblet*' (Gupta 2003: 101), continuing in *Order of the Phoenix* right through to *Deathly Hallows*. Gupta reads the *Harry Potter* series as strongly responding to a current climate in contemporary British society regarding racial purity and inferiority or threat to that purity.

Some critics, such as Jack Zipes and Andrew Blake have viewed the *Harry Potter* books as contributing to racist ideology, given the superiority of the Wizard cultural group over the Muggles. I, however, would contest this, given the contradictory racial impulses at work within the Wizard community, thus attesting to the fact that this is not an idealized culture, but is itself fraught with divisional hierarchies. Another example would be the cause of the House Elves, which is taken up by Hermoine, in her amusing acronym SPEW, though this is problematically not supported by fellow wizards and she is ridiculed for her politicizing of their plight, when their enslaved subservience is portrayed as natural (note that Dumbledore's view coincides with Hermione's on this topic). It is problematic that Wizards are far more powerful than Muggles and, in many ways, control them, but the problems within the Wizard world attest to it being more complex than merely being on the side of Wizards or Muggles, due to both inter-racial unions (remember that Harry himself is half-Muggle, while Hagrid is half-giant), and the divisions existing within Wizards about how they view Muggles. The ultimate power held by the Wizards over the Muggles is part of an inherent cultural issue about the invisibility of a ruling ideology set against marginalized cultural groupings. Society is depicted in a state of perpetual division because of lack of understanding, prejudice and fear among individuals and groups. Feeding on that human negativity and despair are the Dementors, Grim-Reaper-like figures who suck the very soul out of life and threaten to render humanity apathetic automatons. Only through a community-based resistance can such despair and division be overcome and superseded with the hope of a new tomorrow.

Harry epitomizes 'the triumph of good, the power of innocence, the need to keep resisting' (Rowling 2007: 358) that encourages such collective optimism, for, 'We're all still here [. . .] we're still fighting' (Rowling 2007: 522). While clearly a romantic hero (see, for instance, Nikolajeva, [2003]), Harry nevertheless is only as successful as his supporters, indicating that it is the cosmopolitan power of 'we' rather than the patriarchal 'I' that crushes social divisions 'under sheer weight of numbers' (Rowling 2007: 588). Rowling's community is based upon a pluralistic diversity that shares a common goal of overturning Voldemort's death-dealing racial and cultural binaries with the intention of creating a peaceable 'cosmopolitan conviviality' (Gilroy 2004: 9). Defeating Voldemort's melancholically regressive desire for unitary power based on genealogical eugenics – 'The emblem, shield and colours of my noble ancestor, Salazar Slytherin, will suffice for everyone' (Rowling 2007: 586) – Harry establishes a new order based on communal respect for difference. In *Deathly Hallows*, 'nobody was sitting according to house any more: all were jumbled together, teachers and pupils, ghosts and parents, centaurs and house-elves' (Rowling 2007: 597). Far from attempting to erase cultural diversity, Harry inspires understanding between races and social sectors in order to promote the richness of such an abundance of difference. *Deathly Hallows* argues that "[w]e're all human, aren't we? Every human life is worth the same, and worth saving" (Rowling 2007: 357). This cosmopolitan outlook both celebrates human diversity while at the same time urging a reconnection in the face of our common humanity as inhabitants of Earth. Rowling's series is a stark warning against isolationist competitive individualism and an urgency of community cohesion. Discussing 'elf rights', Hermione says, "I mean, it's the same kind of nonsense as werewolf segregation, isn't it? It all stems from this horrible thing wizards have of thinking they're superior to other creatures" (Rowling 2003: 155). Each prejudice, hatred and division is interlinked in the series insofar as you reap what you sow, and that destructive binary cycle can only be broken by the cosmopolitan capacity to love others as well as oneself in a bid to "live and let live" (Rowling 2005: 11). SPEW is not just an amusing acronym but signifies the abject horror of social division that we ignore at the peril of social cohesion, for it demonstrates nauseating hostile difference and urges reconciliation and human empathy: humour is politicized to heighten the absurdity of prejudice and voice disgust at the divisiveness of self/other.

Another problematic cultural hierarchy that is an issue in the novel is gender categorization. Many critics have pointed out that Harry would never achieve as much as he does, both academically and in terms of solving mysteries, if he were not aided by his helpful side-kick, Hermione. Heilman

> hated the way Hermione cowered in fear when faced with the troll, and was disappointed that she had to be rescued by the boys. While Ron and Harry successfully face a horrible twelve-foot-tall troll, Hermione couldn't move [. . .] Hermione had been portrayed as a girl who knew a lot of spells, but when she needed to put that knowledge to use, she failed. (Heilman 2003: 222)

In *Philosopher's Stone*, female passivity and male activity is very clear from the narrator's description: 'Hermione Granger was shrinking against the wall opposite, looking as if she was about to faint' (129), and 'she couldn't move, she was still flat against the wall, her mouth open with terror' (130). It is at this point that both the male characters leap into action, in the vein of chivalric heroes. So Hermione is portrayed as the damsel-in-distress and it is even more stereotypically feminine that, on page 127, we learn that she has been hiding all day and discovered in the girls' toilets crying because of being insulted by Ron for her studiousness. Thus, 'Sometimes females begin an action scene as a token presence, but something always happens to them. Hermione is primarily an enabler of Harry's and Ron's adventures, rather than an adventurer in her own right' (Heilman 2003: 224). In *Chamber of Secrets*, though Hermione perfects the Polyjuice Potion, 'which works fine for Harry and Ron, leading them into further adventures', it fails to work for Hermione. Instead, 'She accidentally turns into a cat, which causes her to sob and pull her robes over her head. She is hospitalized for weeks. In another plot twist, she is later immobilized by being turned into a "petrified person"' (Heilman 2003: 224). Clearly, Hermione is forced constantly into the role of feminized inferior position, where she is removed from the action and placed into a position of inactivity or stasis. But, like the issue of blood, one must ask whether the novels are prescribing this gender-polarized position in which female characters are rendered inactive or merely describe the continuing situation within the wider context of patriarchal society. Similarly, in terms of social class, Ron assists Harry and, while his adventures continue further than Hermione, he is nevertheless denied the full glory of Harry's exploits. As the novels progress, these issues continue, but characters also evolve in the later novels, which tends to address if not fully resolve some of these concerns. Counteracting earlier depictions of females in the series, in *Half-Blood Prince* (2005) Ginny does not cry when Harry must leave her to fight Voldemort but, instead, 'She met Harry's gaze with the same hard, blazing look' (Rowling 2005: 602).

Good and evil seems clear-cut, with Harry and his allies on one side and Voldemort's dark side on the other. But, on closer inspection, Harry himself has the qualities to be in Slytherin according to the Sorting Hat, which was the school of Voldemort and the Malfoys. Voldemort is also half-Muggle like Harry, which makes it more interesting that he is so hateful of half-blood wizards and promotes the racial ideology of pure bloods. Further, the wand Harry buys is discussed by Mr Ollivander, the wand-shop owner, who informs Harry, 'It is very curious indeed that you should be destined for this wand when its brother – why, its brother gave you that scar' (Rowling 1997: 65). As doppelgangers, the line between Harry and Voldemort is often confused and blurred from the first novel and beyond as the series continues. Tom Marvolo Riddle is an anagram of I am Lord Voldemort, and the blurring of that 'I' oscillates between Harry and his alter ego, Voldemort. Dumbledore informs Harry in *Deathly Hallows* that, 'A part of his soul was still attached to yours [. . .] he took a part of your mother's sacrifice into himself [. . .] wrapped your destinies together more securely than ever two wizards were joined in history' (Rowling 2007: 569). Similarly, characters whom we are led to believe are evil, like Slytherin's Snape, end up saving Harry's life, whereas the assumed good character Prof Quirrell is actually one of Voldemort's legion; likewise, Sirius Black is another good character assumed to be evil in *Prisoner of Azkaban*. The mechanics of the narrative followed by Harry in his search for clues to both his own heritage and to the defeat of Voldemort seem to be laid out and engineered by the surrogate father figure of Dumbledore who, we learn, leaves the Mirror of Erised where Harry can find it. He seems to be an all-seeing presence, telling Harry, 'I don't need a cloak to become invisible' (Rowling 1997: 156) as he confesses to having watched over Harry and Ron's clandestine visit to the mirror. He also conveniently disappears on official business just at the point when Harry is in greatest danger and then returns to save the day at the eleventh hour. Harry notes,

> He's a funny man, Dumbledore. I think he sort of wanted to give me a chance. I think he knows more or less everything that goes on here, you know. I reckon he had a pretty good idea we were going to try, and instead of stopping us, he just taught us enough to help. I don't think it was an accident he let me find out how the Mirror worked. It's almost like he thought I had the right to face Voldemort if I could. . . . (Rowling 1997: 219)

Ultimately, Dumbledore could be read as the surrogate father/ author in the text, busily pulling Harry's strings and setting him off on quests until, when Harry must embrace his young manhood, Dumbledore dies.

Voldemort can translate as death-wish, which, of course, corresponds to Freud's death-drive. Often in the series, we learn that Harry desires to die usually because of Voldemort's cruelty, which would, of course, fulfil the Freudian idea of one's desire for the death-drive, which is the desire to return to before we existed with all of the world's pain – that place, of course, is the womb. The Mirror of Erised, of course, involves the desire to return to the idealized mother (Lily represents peace, purity and death). This equates with his quest to defeat Voldemort insofar as it could entail death: so womb and tomb amount to the same thing. As Nicholas Royle points out, 'To recall Freud's formulation, the double is "the uncanny harbinger of death". One may want one's double dead; but the death of the double will always also be the death of oneself' (Royle 2003: 190). Rowling evades this outcome, though, in the final novel. Harry almost dies when he ends up in a state of limbo after defeating Voldemort. In this railway station waiting room, he is briefly reunited with the dead Dumbledore, who tells him that he has a choice in terms of moving on to death or returning to his earthly body. So Harry defeats his doppelganger and, in doing so, kills the part of himself that was Voldemort, thus preserving himself as the romantic hero.

PHILIP PULLMAN – *HIS DARK MATERIALS* (1995–2000)

Philip Pullman's *Northern Lights* was first published in 1995 and in 1996 in the United States under the title of *The Golden Compass*. *Northern Lights* is the first part of the trilogy *His Dark Materials*: the other two novels in the trilogy are *The Subtle Knife*, published in 1997, and ending with *The Amber Spyglass* in 2000 (although a spin-off, related text was published in 2003, called *Lyra's Oxford* and, more recently in 2008, *Once upon a Time in the North*). The trilogy is epic in proportions and vision, and is comparable with Tolkien's *Lord of the Rings* or C.S. Lewis's *Narnia Chronicles* with its consideration of multiple worlds, though Pullman dislikes these particular associations. Pullman believes that Lewis peddles Christian propaganda and suppresses the development of childhood into maturity. According to Pullman, Lewis disallows the move to adolescence and burgeoning sexuality by rigidly maintaining and policing a notion of childhood innocence. Pullman regards his status as a writer in terms of longevity:

> There are many reasons why I write. I write for money and because I would go mad if I didn't. And because I have the not-dishonourable ambition to be famous. And I don't mean famous in the sense of slightly celebrated now, but I mean known in two to three hundred years' time. If you're doing something really well, you should want the results to last that long. (Carter 1999: 185)

He also argues that *His Dark Materials* is not a trilogy insofar as it being three separate books, but that it is one book written in three volumes, which adds to his desire for the work to be seen in epic dimensions. Both in length and structure, the trilogy contains elements of epic, drawing as on John Milton's *Paradise Lost*, and covering not one universe, but several, thus creating a fictional multiverse, where characters weave in and out of several worlds.

This desire for his literature to have staying power in a canonical sense has gotten off to a commendable start. *Northern Lights* was awarded The Carnegie Medal and The Guardian Children's Fiction Award, and won Children's Book of the Year at the British Book Awards. Tellingly, *The Amber Spyglass* won The Whitbread Prize for Fiction – a prestigious award up until this point only given to adult literature, so Pullman's is the first children's book ever to win The Whitbread Prize. It also blurs the boundary between adult and children's fiction, given the epic status of *His Dark Materials* and their dual readership of adults as well as children. Pullman's father died as an RAF fighter pilot in Kenya, leaving Pullman a "half-orphan" as he has put it, and, of course, echoes many of the heroes and heroines of children's stories, including his writing. Interestingly, like Lyra's relationship with her father Lord Asriel, or Will's with his father in *The Subtle Knife*, Pullman's father was a rather glamorous heroic figure, but nevertheless quite distant. Pullman's grandfather was a member of the clergy in the Church of England who, from an early age, introduced him to the Bible but also to the allure of stories, as his grandfather was, in Pullman's words, 'a wonderful storyteller': so he helped to light and fire his creative imagination. Like Lyra in *Northern Lights*, Pullman's knowledge of Oxford is concisely intricate because he studied English at the University of Oxford. *His Dark Materials* is a work of dissent, particularly in relation to its attitudes to institutionalized religion, to childhood and to the tradition of children's literature itself. He weaves a panoramic vision in these works that alludes to mythology, the Bible, Milton's *Paradise Lost*, and to the Romantic poet William Blake's works. In his Acknowledgements in *The Amber Spyglass*, Pullman readily admits, 'I have stolen ideas from every book I have ever read', while the epigraph to *Northern Lights* is from Book II of *Paradise Lost*. Pullman sees *His Dark Materials* as a rewrite of Milton's poem. He says, 'I did *Paradise Lost* at "A" level, and it's stayed with me all the way through until I was beginning to think about *Northern Lights* [. . .] what I really wanted to do was *Paradise Lost* for teenagers' (Carter 1999: 187).

From conception, *Northern Lights* is the first volume of a concept borne out of an intertextual relationship with Milton's poem. Milton's poem *Paradise Lost* is itself a rewrite of the Bible's book of Genesis, involving Satan's expulsion from heaven for attempting to overthrow God, and his resultant temptation of Eve in the Garden of Eden via the Serpent, leading to the Fall of mankind and expulsion from Eden. Each of these earlier texts is a palimpsest overwritten by Pullman's work. What is fascinating about *Paradise Lost*, though, is the way that Satan and Eve are portrayed in a vibrant, lively way, whereas God's character is comparatively dull – the conventional baddies get the best parts written for them and are more interesting (Milton's poem, in turn, is a commentary upon the politics of the historical period in which he is writing, so it is a political allegory). Pullman applies the energy of Milton's response to the original biblical Fall by creating a response to contemporary debates about religion, society and childhood, within the parameters of children's literature. In *Northern Lights* and throughout *His Dark Materials*, Lyra is described as being Eve again – the Scholars had 'chased her away from the fruit trees in the Garden' (Pullman 1995: 19) – and clearly the association to be made is between Lyra's pursuit of knowledge and the forbidden fruit in the Garden of Eden, the capital G emphasizing the significance of the Garden. She is even referred to by the witches as the next Eve.

Another major influence in Pullman's trilogy is William Blake's poetry, particularly *The Marriage of Heaven and Hell*; and *Songs of Innocence and of Experience*. In *The Marriage of Heaven and Hell*, Blake famously wrote in 'The Voice of the Devil' of the unfettering of desire in Milton's *Paradise Lost*, saying that

> Those who restrain Desire, do so because theirs is weak enough to be restrained, and the restrainer or Reason Usurps its place and governs the unwilling. And being restrained, it by degrees becomes passive, till it is only the shadow of Desire. The history of this is written in *Paradise Lost* [. . .] The reason Milton wrote in fetters when he wrote of Angels and God, and at liberty when of Devils and Hell, is because he was a true Poet, and of the Devil's party without knowing it. (Blake 1994 [1790]: 179–80)

Blake sides with the Devil's party consciously – he says that Milton was also of the Devil's party, but unconsciously. By implication, Pullman sees himself as a true poet, a writer of great literature, and associates himself with the Devil's party – those who remain at liberty to creatively speak for themselves, unfettered by the grand narrative of institutionalized religion. This is what Blake referred to as the 'mind-forg'd manacles' in his poem 'London'; or the way that he perceives the oppressive rules and prohibitions of the Church in 'The Garden of Love', where he writes, 'the gates of the Chapel were shut, And "Thou shalt not" writ over the door'. It is this oppressiveness of established religion that Pullman draws upon and focuses on in *Northern Lights* and the other two volumes. In the first part of the trilogy, it states that 'the Church's power over every aspect of life had been absolute' (Pullman 1995: 31). Blake believed that such restraints kept individuals trapped in 'mind forg'd manacles', controlled by religious doctrine, and prevented from reaching their full creative potential. Pullman acknowledges that one of the major influences behind the name of his heroine, Lyra, was Blake. Two poems in his *Songs of Experience* called 'The Little Girl Lost' and 'The Little Girl Found' feature a girl called Lyca, so all Pullman does is to slightly change the name. Lyra's journey in *His Dark Materials* echoes this idea of a little girl who is lost, in the sense that she does not know who she is or what her origins are and then becomes, after an adventurous quest, the little girl found.

Lyra's name is also linked to the constellation Lyra – the group of stars takes its name from Lyre, an ancient stringed instrument, a bit like a small harp. Notably,

> the group of stars commonly referred to as the constellation Lyra has taken on a myriad of different meanings, and has been subject to just as many varying interpretations across cultural boundaries [. . .] The star is also commonly associated with a harp, or known as "the harp star" [. . .] the constellation's prominent alpha star Vega proves its historical significance as a central element in mythological stories of Asian origin. The tale identifies vega as a "weaving girl", in courtship with a neighbouring "herd boy", represented by Altair of the constellation Aquila. The two neglected their duties in the heavens, and were eternally divided by the Celestial River, the Milky Way Galaxy. (http://geology.wcupa.edu/mgagne/ess362/homework/constellations/lyra.htm)

Pullman draws on this myth because Lyra meets Will in *The Subtle Knife* and at the end of *The Amber Spyglass* they become, significantly, star-crossed lovers who must return to their respective universes and lead separate lives, only to be aware of each other's presence by going to the Botanic Garden in their own respective

Oxfords. Pullman's novel is also in keeping with this myth because both Lyra and her love, Will, defy the Authority in heaven in order to fulfil their destinies and create not a tyrannical kingdom, but a 'republic of heaven' (Pullman 2001 [2000]: 548). Lyra is the new Eve and her prophesied Fall is welcomed in the trilogy as the only way to move forward towards knowledge (including sexual knowledge) and enlightenment and to celebrate the consciousness symbolized through Dust. This association between Lyra the little girl and the constellation is further emphasized because the constellation is regarded as small in size but very significant – just as Lyra in the novel is only a child but phenomenally important in the multiple universes of the text. Her journey in the final chapter, poignantly called 'The Bridge to the Stars', takes her into the heavenly realm towards the Northern Lights and into Citagazze, the world encountered in *The Subtle Knife*. The first volume concludes, 'So Lyra and her daemon turned away from the world they were born in, and looked towards the sun, and walked into the sky' (Pullman 1995: 399). Lyra and the musical instrument, the lyre, are very similar to the word 'liar' – in the novels Lyra constantly makes up stories and, in the final part of the trilogy, the harpy 'No-Name' spells this out for us by repeating her name until '*Lyra* and *liar* were one and the same thing' (Pullman 2000: 308).

The title of the first volume, *Northern Lights* is worthy of consideration. The trilogy itself, called *His Dark Materials* is directly taken from Book II of Milton's *Paradise Lost* and is mentioned in the epigraph, and is used by Pullman in order to apply his metaphor of Dust from the Dark Matter of the universe. The Northern Lights is the common name for the Aurora Borealis, an astronomical phenomenon found in the Northern Hemisphere, which is a bit like a heavenly light show. In the first novel, Lord Asriel is experimenting with this phenomenon in the North beyond Lapland. Lord Asriel refers directly to this, mentioning 'a certain natural phenomenon only seen in the lands of the North' (Pullman 1995: 21) and 'It's a picture of the Aurora [. . .] the Northern Lights' (Pullman 1995: 23). Like most heavenly phenomena, the Northern Lights have been the subject of much mythology and folklore and are a gift for a writer who draws on cultural myths, as Pullman does. The way in which Lord Asriel describes the world in the Aurora is drawing on the idea that, at times, it looks like in thinner parts of the light structure, that there is a bridge. That is the bridge Lyra crosses to ascend into the sky at the end of the first volume. A scientific explanation is that they are a phenomena generated by the sun's 'high-energy charged particles (also called ions)' that form a cloud 'called a plasma. The stream of plasma coming from the sun is known as the solar wind'. When the solar wind reaches 'the edge of the earth's magnetic field, some of the particles are trapped by it and they follow the lines of magnetic force down into the ionosphere, the section of the earth's atmosphere that extends from about 60 to 600 kilometres above the earth's surface'. The interaction of these particles with the ionosphere's gases causes them to glow, 'producing the spectacle that we know as the auroras, northern and southern. The array of colours consists of red, green, blue and violet' (http://virtual.finland. fi/finfo/english/aurora_borealis.html). However, folklore abounds on the subject. For example,

> Some cultures, especially those at high latitudes, have regarded the sighting of the aurora as a sign of royal birth; to others it suggests ghosts of the dead or the precursor for war [. . .] Up until the Enlightenment of the eighteenth century, the northern lights often were viewed with fear or reverence and were related to contemporary concepts of heaven and hell. (http://webexhibits.org/ causesofcolor/4C.html)

Clearly, Pullman draws on both scientific theory of quantum physics and extensive folklore in order to create a complex intertextual epic tale. In terms of 'royal birth', notice that Lyra as the next Eve is the saviour of humanity. The cultural superstition that the aurora could be connected ominously to war is, of course, one of the strands that run through Pullman's trilogy. The very first mention made of Lord Asriel is associated in Lyra's mind with such concepts, for 'He was said to be involved in high politics, in secret exploration, in distant warfare' (6), while the concepts of heaven and hell are major concerns in the text.

That battle culminates in the epic struggle to reclaim power from the Authority of the Church, finally culminating the embodiment of the philosopher Friedrich Neitzsche's claim that 'God is dead', insofar as he is merely a projection that fills a hole in human need which, ultimately, only serves to weigh us down and hold us back intellectually. In *The Amber Spyglass*, the archaic reign of the church is represented through a frail, out of touch God, who merely blows away in the wind. The Aurora Borealis takes its name from Greek Goddess of the Dawn, Aurora. As Lyra is so closely associated with heavenly bodies and has a mission to fulfil in the trilogy as the new Eve, it is clear that her role is to herald in a new dawn, in the sense that she brings freedom and hope to humanity. The witches point out that, 'Without this child, we shall all die' (Pullman 1998 [1995]: 175–6). When Lyra looks at the aurora borealis, there is a sense that her journey towards wisdom is underway and the notion of what is holy is challenged. Rather than the established church being holy, it is regarded as corrupt. Instead, astral phenomena and natural wonders like the northern lights offer spiritual sustenance. By looking at them, Lyra experiences an epiphany:

As if from Heaven itself, great curtains of delicate light hung and trembled [. . .] fiery crimson like the fires of Hell, they swung and shimmered loosely [. . .] she felt something as profound [. . .] She was moved by it: it was so beautiful it was almost holy; she felt tears prick her eyes, and the tears splintered the light even further into prismatic rainbows [. . .] And as she gazed, the image of a city seemed to form itself behind the veils and streams of translucent colour. (Pullman 1998 [1995]: 183)

Her awakening allows her to see beyond the veiled myopic gaze of polarized society and into the spectrum of new, hitherto unexplored possibilities. In that awakening, we witness not a divisive binary between heaven and hell as with normative society but, rather, a marriage of heaven and hell.

Pullman aligns himself with a creative school of thought, which like Blake's, is consciously on the side of the Devil's Party, or the rebels, against the straight-jacketing of the Church and its repressive mind controls. Instead, Pullman advocates the absolute necessity for the artist to be able to create freely, unbound by any social controls or censorships: only then, he argues, can true artist expression take place. In his acceptance speech for the Carnegie Medal, which he won for *Northern Lights*, Pullman said,

All stories teach, whether the storyteller intends them to or not. They teach the world we create. They teach the morality we live by. They teach it more effectively than moral precepts and instructions [. . .] We don't need lists of rights and wrongs, tables of do's and don'ts: we need books, time, and silence. Thou shalt not is soon forgotten, but Once upon a time lasts forever. (www.delanet.com/~ftise/pullman.html)

Pullman sees himself as a storyteller and, for him, the power of the story is everything. In that sense the title of the trilogy could refer to the art and tools of the storyteller himself, as well as to Lord Asriel's rebellious science. Although *His Dark Materials* has been generally very well received, Pullman's outspokenness and clear anti-theologian stance in the trilogy has led to counterattack from conservative supporters of the Church. For example, Peter Hitchens declared in the *Mail on Sunday* that Pullman is 'the most dangerous author in Britain'. The journalist, Claudia Fitzherbets wrote, 'Christian parents beware: his books can damage your child's faith'. Michael Dirda suggests, with reference to *The Amber Spyglass* that, 'In another time, this is a book that would have made the Index [the Catholic list of prohibited texts], and in still another era gotten its author condemned to the stake as a heretic' (Squires 2003: 72–3). Pullman's dialectic trilogy that engages with the repressive control of Western society, underpinned with Christian doctrine, has evoked exactly the kind of response considered in his text.

Pullman's teaching in these three novels echoes the arguments espoused by the Marxist critic, Louis Althusser, where he argues that 'in Marxist theory, the State Apparatus (SA) contains: the Government, the Administration, the Army, the Police, the Courts, the Prisons, etc., which constitute what I shall in future call the Repressive State Apparatus' (Easthope and McGowan 1992: 50–1). More subtly, 'Ideological State Apparatuses (ISAs)' include 'a certain number of realities' presented 'in the form of distinct and specialized institutions [. . .] the religious ISA (the system of the different Churches), the educational ISA [. . .] the family ISA, the legal ISA, the political ISA' (Easthope and McGowan 1992: 50–1), for example. He continues, 'What distinguishes the ISAs from the (Repressive) State Apparatus is [. . .] the Repressive State Apparatus functions "by violence", whereas the Ideological State Apparatuses *function* "by *ideology*"' (Easthope and McGowan 1992: 50–1). Pullman's Authority can be seen in terms of Althusser's view of the way in which ideology functions to construct a particular sense of reality, through controlling a society's collective mind. Likewise, for Karl Marx, 'Religion is the sigh of the oppressed creature, the sentiment of a heartless world and the soul of soulless conditions. It is the *opium* of the people.' (O'Malley 2007 [1994]: 57). Pullman wants to open his readers' eyes, to demystify them by offering alternative possibilities and realities that challenge the constrained Grand Narratives of Western culture. Pullman blurs rigid boundaries or Western binaries by setting much of *Northern Lights* in the North Pole – the final section of the novel is set in Svalbard, an extreme North region of the Arctic, owned by Norway. The North Pole is regarded as a place without boundaries or borders – the shifting magnetic Pole. 'The magnetic poles are not fixed but follow circular paths with diameters of about 100 miles (160 km). Studies of paleomagnetism also indicate that the earth's magnetic field has reversed its polarity many times in the geologic past' (www.answers.com/topic/north-pole).

Northern Lights concerns itself with the spatial concept of boundaries and ways in which these can be rendered porous. From the outset, Lyra is introduced to us as an unconventional heroine in the sense that she transgresses traditional demarcations. She is of noble birth (her father is Lord Asriel), yet she is also an illegitimate child, and she crosses class barriers, given that her closest friend is the kitchen-boy, Roger. Similarly, she subverts gender binaries in her association with male friends and her active masculine pursuits, such as climbing the roof of Oxford University, befriending street children, participating in gang battles, smoking, drinking and, finally, setting off on a quest to rescue her abducted male friend, Roger, as well as her imprisoned father. So boundaries between male/female, privileged/poor, adult/child are continually disrupted through the very strong and active heroine, Lyra. She is also a rebellious female child in the sense that she invades a traditional academic adult male space. The oppressive sense of patriarchal tradition hangs heavy in the air, with 'Portraits of former Masters hung high up in the gloom along the walls' (3), and into this heavily static space comes the sprightly movement of a new generation. This scene echoes Virginia Woolf's polemical essay, *A Room of One's Own* in which she satirizes the absurdity of male academic traditional authority, where women are ostracized. Although surrounded by educated males, Woolf, like Lyra at this point, also did not receive a formal education. It is interesting that Lyra is referred to later in the trilogy as the new Eve, destined to create the second Fall, and she begins her journey of rebellion from innocence towards knowledge at the very seat of knowledge, in the form of Jordan College, Oxford. Like her namesake Lyca in Blake's poems, Lyra is the little girl lost insofar as she is ignorant of the path she is about to embark upon, and then becomes the little girl found as she attains wisdom. Pullman summarizes his trilogy by describing it in terms of a shift from naïve innocence to the maturity of experience, including, sexual experience, as witnessed in *The Amber Spyglass*. Pullman argues that

> Traditionally, children are seen as beautiful, innocent beings; then comes adulthood and they become corrupt. That's the C.S. Lewis view. My view is that the coming of experience and sexuality and self-consciousness is a thing to be welcomed, because it's the beginning of true understanding, of wisdom. My book tells children that you're going to grow up and it's going to be painful but it's going to be good too. (Walsh 2003: 247)

So, for Pullman, the journey is not so much Blake's view of innocence to experience, but ignorance to wisdom and self-knowledge. As far as boundaries go, this is the most pivotal aspect of his trilogy, the oscillation between innocence and wisdom. In biblical terms of the original Fall in the Garden of Eden, Pullman regards Lyra's role in positive, welcome, necessary terms as the Fortunate Fall, or *felix culpa*. As Millicent Lenz points out, 'Not until the fourth century C.E. did Eve's quest for knowledge begin to be viewed as (like Pandora's curiosity) the source of humanity's woes.' (Lenz 2005: 159). It is only through this move towards enlightenment that the darkness of humanity will be removed as the 'mind forg'd manacles' are unlocked. What he is doing as a writer is to challenge the traditions of children's literature, which maintains childhood in a perpetual state of prelapsarian ignorance. Mary Harry Russell argues that 'Pullman fits comfortably into the position of a Gnostic outsider, interrogating authority' (Lenz 2005: 212). Eve will always be open to interpretation, Russell posits 'since Genesis 1:3 is a text so filled with contradictions' and 'Especially in the early decades of Christianity, at a period of time when neither the Hebrew nor the Christian canons were fixed, there was considerable literary activity, in authoring and preserving a variety of texts about the events of the Creation and Fall' (Lenz 2005: 213). As such, '"The situation of early Christianity was simply much more fluid – indeed, confused – than has been acknowledged" [. . .] the dissident writers we now characterize as Gnostic [. . .] can frequently be seen seeking a different explanation for the events in Eden.' (Lenz 2005: 213–14).

Pullman, as an Oxford graduate, follows in the footsteps of fellows Oxford men Lewis Carroll, C.S. Lewis and J.R.R. Tolkien, but, like Lyra, Pullman wants to dispense with tradition (particularly Lewis) by creating a new type of children's literature that resists these earlier mindsets. Perhaps he is paying some kind of homage to Carroll's anarchic writing when Lyra assumes the identity of 'Alice' (101) to fend off a strange man attempting to put brandy in the coffee he buys for her, signalling the strange Wonder-Land of London which she finds herself lost in. It's described as 'a tangle of narrow streets [. . .] that dark maze (99), and 'She had no idea where she was, because she had never seen a map of London, and she didn't even know how big it was or how far she'd have to walk to find the country' (101). One of the witches refers to this necessary rebellion when she talks of Lord Asriel in *The Subtle Knife*. She says, 'He showed me that to rebel was right and just [. . .] And I thought of the Bolvangar children, and the other terrible mutilations I have seen in our own south-lands; and he told me of many more hideous cruelties dealt out in the Authority's name – of how they capture witches, in some worlds, and burn them alive, sisters, yes, witches like ourselves [. . .] He opened my eyes. He showed me things I never had seen, cruelties and horrors all committed in the name of the Authority, all designed to destroy the joys and truthfulness of life' (Pullman 1997: 283).

Insofar as he is responsible for opening people's eyes through his rebellion against the Church, Lord Asriel is very much akin to the figure of Milton's Satan in *Paradise Lost*. Notably, Ariel (which is similar to Asriel) was one of the rebellious angels in Milton's epic poem. Lord Asriel, like so many other aspects of these books, is a character who crosses boundaries of what could be perceived as good and evil. In many ways, he is the Byronic hero of the texts in the sense that he has a dark, yet intoxicating appeal, and is rebellious. The hero/villain dichotomy in literature is inverted here as Asriel is engaged in a heroic struggle against the Authority, yet simultaneously displays darker qualities and is responsible for the death of Lyra's friend, Roger. Mary Malone, the ex-nun turned scientist turned environmentalist, is cast in the role of the tempting serpent in *The Amber Spyglass* and she explains her shift from relying upon a closed way of thinking in religious doctrine, to embracing and trusting in her own morality and knowledge. She says,

> I stopped believing there was a power of good and a power of evil that were outside us. And I came to believe that good and evil are names for what people do, not for what they are. All we can say is that this is a good deed, because it helps someone, or that's an evil one, because it hurts them. People are too complicated to have simple labels. (Pullman 2000: 470–1)

In this trilogy Pullman does not paint a world of despair without the guidelines of the authoritative church; instead his novels offer hope in individuals to be able to function in collective societies with their own measures of moral behaviour. Mrs Coulter, like Asriel, demonstrates darker qualities – we particularly respond to her negatively because of her lack of maternal qualities: she is the epitome of the femme fatale insofar as she is a very attractive yet very deadly woman. But, by the final part of the trilogy she demonstrates some redeeming maternal qualities, finally sacrificing herself for the future of both her daughter, Lyra, and the human race (Asriel dies at this point too) in its fight against the Authority's tyranny. Mrs Coulter's involvement with the Experimental Station at Bolvangar is apt because, like the guillotine used to sever child and daemone, her surname means cutter. This severance experiment between pre-pubescent child and its demon echoes Western cultural history with its 'shades of the Mengelian horrors of the Nazi era' (Hunt and Lenz 2001: 127). Crucially, the vast majority of children taken to Bolvangar are vagrants, while those who run the Experimental Centre, who also have been separated from their daemons are 'adults who make perfect cogs in a war machine. The verbal associations with "The Killing Fields" and the surgical operation known as "lobotomy" in our own world underscore Pullman's social/political criticism of "real" world atrocities' (Hunt and Lenz 2001: 131). This, of course, signals ways in which fantasy children's literature can engage with reality rather than be remote from it.

The way in which the adults at Bolvangar demonstrate their lack of curiosity or enthusiasm for life is a future vision of what will happen to the younger generation, if they, too, are surgically prevented from reaching the maturity of experience by being severed from their daemons. It is like a polar binary in which self and other are separated, as childhood is forever maintained rigidly separate from knowledge. When Mrs Coulter hypocritically tries to justify the guillotine process to Lyra, she says, ' "The nurses seem happy enough, don't they?" Lyra blinked. Suddenly she understood their strange blank incuriosity, the way their little trotting daemons seemed to be sleepwalking' (Pullman 1995: 284). At this point, Lyra sees Mrs Coulter's lies clearly, as though a veil has been lifted from her eyes, she 'wondered how she had ever, ever, ever found this woman to be so fascinating and clever'. (Pullman 1995: 286). The intercision process is also dominated by social class, given that the majority of children kidnapped by the Oblation Board or Gobblers tend to be on the impoverished fringes of society. Again, Pullman appears to be using children's fantasy fiction in order to provide poignant social commentary. In 1997 *BBC News* reported that, 'In the 1980s the world was shocked to learn of the murder of street children in Rio de Janeiro, often by policemen determined to wipe out what they saw as a social nuisance. These killings still go on' (http://news.bbc.co.uk/1/hi/despatches/americas/25908.stm).

In a conversation about Lyra with Lee Scoresby, the witch Serafina Pekkala says:

> We are all subject to the fates. But we must all act as if we are not [. . .] or die of despair. There is a curious prophecy about this child: she is destined to bring about the end of destiny. But she must do so without knowing what she is doing, as if it were her nature and not her destiny to do it. If she's told what she must do, it will all fail; death will sweep through all the worlds; it will be the triumph of despair, for ever. The universes will all become nothing more than interlocking machines, blind and empty of thought, feeling, life. . . . (Pullman 1995: 310)

In other words, the universes will become as unthinking and incurious as the nurses at Bolvangar, as the Blakean 'mind forg'd manacles' remain firmly shackled around creative potential. As a creator himself, Pullman strives to encourage his readers to question and challenge the Truths they are told in life in the name of Grand Narratives or Authority, and to see through these discourses. By doing so, the creative potential of His Dark Materials is unleashed, allowing people to see beyond the rigidity of Western so-called reality. The idea of seeing through the veil is important, as Lyra does when she realizes her mother is not who she hoped she was, or when the possible of alternative worlds can be seen in the thin veil of the Northern Lights. Just as in the astronomical phenomenon of the Northern Lights, Pullman wants his literary phenomenon Northern Lights to illuminate the power of creativity and wonder in his reader. A key theme in Pullman's novel and wider trilogy is the pursuit of and quest for knowledge. While regarded as going against biblical doctrine, it is interesting to point out that the proverbs teach us the importance of wisdom rather than ignorance: 'For wisdom *is* better than rubies; and all the things that may be desired are not to be compared to it [. . .] Forsake the foolish, and live; and go in the way of understanding' (Proverbs 8.11 and 9.6). This is an incorporation into biblical thinking from earlier Aristotelian philosophy. Aristotle believed that '[h]uman life was defined by its end of "living well." And living well was defined as exercising one's highest capacity – wisdom – in order to form one's life into a stable and coherent whole' (Colebrook 2004: 22). Plato's *The Republic* (notice that Lord Asriel wants to build not a Kingdom but a Republic of Heaven) argues that individuals exist metaphorically in a dark cave, mistaking the illusive puppet-show shadows visible on the cave wall for reality. Only the few Guardians, he argues, have the courage to leave the cave, attaining enlightened wisdom and understanding. Thus, 'Plato pictures human life as a pilgrimage from appearance to reality.' (Murdoch 1978: 2). In *The Amber Spyglass* Lyra and Will, as Guardians of wisdom, descend into a cave in order to bring the dead in the underworld back to rest in peace within their earthly home.

JULIE BERTAGNA – *EXODUS* (2002) AND *ZENITH* (2007)

Exodus is the first part of a trilogy by Julie Bertagna. The sequel *Zenith* was published in 2007 and the final instalment, *Aurora* will be published in 2011. Just finished being written, it is absolutely contemporary: as young-adult fiction, *Exodus* shows a growth in childhood developed within children's literature since the First Golden Age. A work of fantasy, the theoretical models of, for instance, Jackson and Armitt discussed earlier are applicable. M.O. Grenby says that 'Fantasy, we find, is not an escape from reality but, often, a rewriting of it' (Grenby 2008: 154). Theoretical frameworks point out that it is powerful and political, and demonstrate clearly that fantasy writers of children's fiction are not attempting to provide a safe and comfortable escapism, and certainly Bertagna is engaging politically in her work. She offers a response on many levels to the anxieties and issues that are all too real in contemporary society.

Bertagna is part of a growing body of writers who use Glasgow as a literary setting: it had traditionally been perceived as somewhere not focused upon in literature, as is made clear in Alasdair Gray's *Lanark*. Like Gray, however, Bertagna's futuristic dystopia adds the twist of fantasy. Discussing Scottish writing, she says, 'I was wrong too about Scotland being ordinary. I find inspiration for stories in the world right outside my window as much as in the world beyond. All you have to do is open your eyes and mind' (www.juliebertagna.com/start.html). Bertagna also follows the trend of contemporary writers like Pullman and Rowling, who resist keeping their child heroes locked in the ignorant naivety of childhood. In that sense, her fiction is part of a relatively new type of children's literature known as Young-Adult fiction that bridges the gap between fiction for children and fiction for adults. Also referred to as Crossover fiction, it is an in-between stage, where the child hero is developing a sense of their emerging adult identity. Often that involves traumatic rites of passage, with all the growing pains of taking responsibility in a heroic role and stepping out of one's comfort zone of familiarity to face the fear of the unknown. Only by doing this can the hero, or in Bertagna's case, the heroine, truly develop. Of course, like Pullman and Rowling, Bertagna's fiction attracts a lot of adult readers – so it is crossover fiction that dissolves the boundaries between the categories of adult and children's texts. Like Pullman, too, Bertagna often uses allusions to other literary texts: for instance, before each section of the novel there is an epigraph from Emily Bronte or from Dante. Cleary, these epigraphs relate in some way to the narrative but, also, it places Bertagna's work within an established literary continuum. It is not a text, then, that we are meant to treat lightly.

The title of the first part of the trilogy, *Exodus*, has connotations of the biblical exodus of the Israelites to the Promised Land. Indeed, the idea of an exodus or journey is a central motif in this trilogy. It features a reluctant heroine, Mara, who, due to the rapidly rising sea levels that are threatening to engulf her island home of Wing, is forced to go on a quest to locate a new home for her people. The rising sea level is caused by an all too real issue, namely of climate change and the shrinking polar ice caps. What Bertagna's novel presents through a futuristic dystopia is the likely outcome to our present global crisis, where already people are beginning to become climate refugees or environmental refugees in some parts of the world. The message within her novel is highly political and challenging: in this novel, the Earth's resources have been plundered for the sake of economic expansion and human development. The Earth has not been regarded as humanity's home that, therefore, must be protected and symbiotically inhabited. Instead, it has been regarded as a store cupboard to be consumed. The preface begins the novel with the sense of telling a story, thus: '*Once upon a time there was a world . . .* '. That world, we're told is Earth, and '[t]*he people feasted upon their ripe world. Endlessly, they harvested its lands and seas. They grew greedy, ravaging the planet's bounty of miracles. Their waste and destruction spread like a plague* [. . .] *And the people saw, too late, their savage desolation of the world.*' Bertagna makes this futuristic disaster immediately relevant to her young-adult reader – she asks, '*Is this where we stand now, right here on the brink?*' (Bertagna 2003 [2002]).

While this is a work of fantasy, it is clearly responding to a current, politically contentious issue that Bertagna feels very passionate about. One of the major problems is that territory and space in terms of national borders will come under increasing pressure as populations are forced to flee rising tides. So,

Amid predictions that by 2010 the world will need to cope with as many as 50 million people escaping the effects of creeping environmental deterioration, United Nations University experts say the international community urgently needs to define, recognize and extend support to this new category of 'refugee' because 'Environmental refugees' are not yet recognized in world conventions. (www.environmentalrefugee.org/facts.html#)

On her website, Bertagna cites an article from *The Guardian* newspaper, stating that,

The majority of the British public doesn't believe that climate change is caused by humans [. . .] Yet a report last year by more than 2,500 scientists for the UN Inter-governmental Panel on

Climate Change found a 90 per cent chance that humans were the main cause of climate change. Drastic action, they said, was needed to cut greenhouse gas emissions. (www.juliebertagna. com/start.html)

Bertagna continues,

> '*Kiribati – a former British colony called the Gilbert Islands* [. . .] *is regarded as one of the places most vulnerable to climate change.* Kiribati was my inspiration for Mara's drowning island in EXODUS. I first read about the Kiribati islands in 1999. Almost a decade on, we, the outside world still have done nothing to help.' (www.juliebertagna.com/start.html)

In terms of fantasy commenting on the real world, Bertagna sets her climate disaster in the year 2099, so that the narrative can then look back at what led to the current impasse. Mara's generation's lives are thwarted by the devastating irresponsibility of their forefathers who, of course, reflect the current situation of ignorance and denial. We learn that:

> In the scorching hot summers of the '30s and '40s the oceans rose faster than anyone ever expected. All the predictions had been wrong. And all the political agreements that were supposed to prevent global warming had long fallen through. The world's governments couldn't seem to agree on anything – or stick to any treaties that they did manage to agree on. Suddenly it was all too late. Great floods struck, all over the world [. . .] Governments began to collapse everywhere. Economies crashed and everything that held society together started to fall apart. (195)

This description offers a terse warning to myopic environmental politics in an increasingly globalized world that must depend upon neighbourly collaboration among all nations to sustain ecological balance. Notice that in Mara's forefather's world, civilization's thin veneer has 'started to fall apart' and is all too easily swept away, like the receding landscape. In Bertagna's vision the preservation of national interests has been achieved at the expense of common supranational denominators. In *Zenith*, the sequel, we witness

Mara and her generation judging their ancestors' culpability: 'They knew. They could've done something but they didn't. They knew. They didn't think about the future, did they? They never thought about us' (206–7). With constant references to our own contemporary debates on global ecology, international politics and an uncertain future, Bertagna positions her readers into confronting the harrowing consequences of doing nothing. According to John Stephens,

> Writing for children is usually purposeful, its intention being to foster in the child reader a positive apperception of some socio-cultural values which [. . .] are shared by author and audience. These values include contemporary morality and ethics, a sense of what is valuable in the culture's past [. . .] and aspirations about the present and future. (Stephens 1992: 3)

In many ways, then, the text is serving as a warning to young-adults who will, of course, *be* the future generation of adults that, if they blindly follow their forefathers, then this fictional scenario might well prove all too prophetically real. Bertagna's young-adult texts motivate a future generation to identify with the collective responsibility of educating themselves and others and confronting the consequences of one's actions. Reflecting our contemporary world's global intolerance for asylum seekers and refugees, Bertagna demonstrates nationalist hegemonies at work, just as she underscores the destructiveness of the nationalist myths of sovereign control and self-reliance. While individual countries continue to monitor their borders, it is clear that if each country fails to think beyond its margins and contribute to a global effort at cutting carbon emissions, then all humanity may potentially wind up as climate refugees, similar to those languishing outside New Mungo's closed imperial fortress (McCulloch 2007a: 69–96). Similarly, Ulrich Beck identifies the importance of a 'cosmopolitan Europe' as a necessity against what he terms 'world risk society' (Beck 2007 [2004]: 176). He says, 'If governments and peoples continue to confine themselves to hermetic national spaces' rather than engaging in the dialogue of cosmopolitan cooperation to overcome global risks, 'then ever more countries and cultures will sink into chaos and decline' (Beck 2007 [2004]: 176–7). Bertagna has tapped into a very relevant current debate, not only regarding climate change but, in turn, the necessity to rethink national borders and embrace cosmopolitan cooperation.

As a 15-year-old, Mara is at a crucial threshold between leaving her childhood behind and entering a new state of adulthood. Bertagna, then, equates Mara's changing body and developing mind as a positive move away from innocent childhood and its naïve lack of responsibility. Instead, Mara must learn through her journey both about her own potential and the culpability of humanity for the state of the drowned Earth that she now inhabits. Her quest takes her from the relative insularity of her small and rapidly diminishing island community to Glasgow, but this is not a recognizable Glasgow. Instead, as a futuristic eco-novel, it is set in a dystopian Glasgow that is now submerged due to the flooding caused by accelerated climate change. This new environmental climate signals a new political climate insofar as the conventional male hero is superseded by a heroine, whose personal destiny is identical to her responsibility to save the nation. Any sense of future in this world is extremely fragile, and the burden of cultural self-preservation lies entirely with the new generation who must heed the mistakes of the past in order to move forward. Mara's pressing desire is that she will 'find a new home in the world' (Bertagna 2003 [2002]: 14) to safeguard her immediate community and the wider nation. Her own vision and determination must be strong enough to overcome her community's fear that there may not be anywhere else to go. In a futuristic eco-novel set in a dystopian Glasgow, now submerged due to the destruction caused by accelerated climate change, it is to be expected that conventions will shift.

In this "new political climate" the conventional male hero is superseded by a heroine, whose personal destiny is identical with her responsibility to save the nation. As such, Bertagna is very much responding in this fantasy to what Margery Hourihan (1997) identifies as being vital for the future of children's literature. Hourihan argues that the traditional boy hero, identified in, for instance, boy's adventure stories, tended to control his surroundings and impose a masculinist authority. While a strong heroine, Mara's status as a young emerging woman inevitably pits her individual story against a whole generic tradition of male heroic-quest narratives. Unsurprisingly, therefore, without any female role models to look up to or model herself after, Mara suffers moments of acute

TEXTS

self-doubt, which threaten to entrap her and thus seriously hinder her mission. So, she says,

> *Maybe I could get out of this. Maybe I could persuade Fox to forget it all. We could let the cyberflood come and do nothing. We could live together and have a nice, snug life here in the New World. Why do I have to be the big heroine? Why me? I don't want it to be me. I'm too scared. I'm just an ordinary girl and all I want is an ordinary life. It's not up to me to save the world.* (303–4)

She must resist this clear patriarchal interpellation into becoming 'ordinary' by internalizing a strictly feminine role in society. What saves her from this is the strength of memory by recalling her dead mother's words: '*I believe in you*' (304). She remembers, too, all those women whose lives have been erased and written out of history, so creating her own female tradition. So, 'She thinks of Granny Mary, who fought so hard in her youth to build a future when it seemed there was none . . . She thinks of Candleriggs, then of Thenew . . . all of them salvaged a future out of the wreckage of their young lives' (304). Bertagna, then, enables her young-adult readers to identify with a strong female character in the hope that they will carry this identification out into the world beyond the text. Hourihan (1997) points out that stories confining girls and women to domesticity have a detrimental ideological impact. Bertagna's fiction challenges the myth of female domesticity by breaking the paralysing stronghold of feminine passivity in a young woman's imagination and replacing it with images of a strong, active female leader.

Bertagna's novel also offers a stark warning against insularity – if you fail to look beyond your borders, then you will become extinct, which forces a geographical as well as psychological shift in the concept of home. Like her small island home and, indeed Scotland itself, Mara is just an insignificant child, yet her actions prove to be of immense importance. Cairns Craig comments not only on the mutual narrative interdependence of individual and communal lives, but also the willingness of individuals to give the welfare of the nation priority over their own personal interests, to the extent of seeing their own life-story assimilated into the narrative of the nation. 'People would act and would sacrifice themselves for the *national* good in ways that they would never act or sacrifice themselves for purely personal ends,' Craig writes, 'because the narrative

131

of the nation and the narrative of their own existence are imaginatively intertwined' (Craig 1999: 10). Likewise, Bertagna's 15-year-
old heroine Mara Bell's destiny becomes fused with her people's
destiny. Bertagna's novels express a particularly urgent need for
'continuity with a founding past' (Craig 1999: 11) to counteract the
traumatic presence of a New World in which the past has undergone 'a culture of erasure' (Craig 1999: 19).

Bertagna's characters go beyond national frontiers to embrace
a supranational or cosmopolitan citizenship. *Exodus* imagines the
nation as a cosmopolitan community insofar as Mara's people must
recognize and tolerate cultural diversity in order to build a home
for themselves that exceeds narrowly nationalist forms of alle-
giance and instead participates in a wider pluralistically organized
world. For Bertagna it is imperative that post-devolution Scotland
should take the opportunity to open up its borders within an
outward-looking inclusive Europe and, indeed, wider globalization
as a whole, reflecting also Eleanor Bell's stance that 'it is important that we now view Scotland and Scottishness as, in part, the
products of globalism, multiculturalism and consumerism in order
to see that we are now "somewhere else entirely"' (Bell 2004: 89).
Cosmopolitan communication is vital in an ever-shrinking world
which 'is getting more crowded' (Appiah 2007 [2006]: xix), just as
Bertagna charts the effect of global demographic pressure.

On her travels, which are set both in the corporeal world and
the figurative realm of cyberspace, Mara encounters a number of
different cultures that help her to expand her own intellectual hori-
zons and carry her new knowledge forward to lay the foundations
of a hybrid state. '[Mara] is looking at the world with eyes wide
open,' writes Bertagna, 'and she is almost sure that there is something out there. A New World, a haven above the seas. A future'
(Bertagna 2003 [2002]: 53). In this futuristic world virtual reality
is a forum for the individual to connect with others in order to
transcend incapacitating regional isolation and envision the revolutionary liberty of a future, for '*in cyberspace there are no rules,
no limits. Anything might happen . . . the Weave is wild and savage*'
(27– 8). Mara first encounters her future partner Fox (his cyber
name)/David (his real name) in the Weave, where only their minds
and stories can meet. Through her relationship with Fox/David she
discovers unknown territory, and it is the Weave that allows the two
young people to forge a relationship that is mutually beneficial.

Like Alice's descent down the rabbit-hole, Mara falls from a crumbling cyber bridge '*into dark, unknown regions of cyberspace. She has fallen right out of the Weave*' (29). In discovering an uncharted alien space on the outer rim of the familiar, Mara and Fox are able to utilize the gap to exchange knowledge and stories about their own cultures: 'This is not the Weave. This is the unknown . . . like something out of a fairy tale' (31). Preconceived notions of reality are irrevocably altered as they begin to learn about alternative cultures: '*How does a cyberfox know about realworld,*' Mara asks Fox, '*are you real?*' (32–3). The in-between crevices of cyberspace allow the young people to interact in radically new ways and move towards a cosmopolitan culture: cyberspace allows for spatial interconnections to open up between characters previously ignorant of the existence of other cultures.

According to Bertagna's representation the old patriarchal society's response to cataclysmic disaster consisted of building insular neo-states – the 'New World sky cities' (*Exodus* 2003 [2002]: 195) – whose phallic architectural excesses towered high above the drowned earth. These arrogant monolithic structures symbolize an elitism that only admitted those deemed suitable and left the rest of society to rot in the polluted waters of the Netherworld. The walls surrounding New Mungo (the sky city built to replace Glasgow) metaphorically denote the border dividing the privileged from society's abject and dispensable who are described as 'the vile, rotting stench' and 'a heaving mass of humanity' that 'clings like a fungus to the huge wall' (*Exodus*: 66). The abject, according to Julia Kristeva is that part of ourselves that we do not wish to acknowledge and, in Bertagna's novel, it is the part of humanity that New Mungo is trying to render invisible. Enraged by this injustice and systematic dehumanization, Fox acknowledges that '*this* is what [this] world does. Kills children like vermin when they get in the way' (Bertagna 2007: 281). As she breaks out of the Netherworld and into the world of elitist privilege, Mara begins to question how people manage to live in the sterile environment of New Mungo. 'Are the people of the sky city so bedazzled by their glittering New World that they can't see beyond it to the human catastrophe right outside their wall' (Bertagna 2003 [2002]: 72), she wonders. 'Do they not know what is happening? But somebody knows, because somebody built that city wall' (Bertagna 2003 [2002]: 72). New Mungo has a distorted vision, 'which builds its empire out of such cruelty and decides its citizens are the only true human beings in the world – that the rest of us are no better than vermin' (Bertagna 2003 [2002]: 192). Eventually, the outward-looking supranational citizens of Scotland's future, led by Mara and her sky-city lover Fox, disrupt New Mungo's dystopian world to allow a hopeful future to emerge.

New Mungo is created by Fox's grandfather, Caledon. In Caledon's world, everything is artificial and Mara sees through its surface veneer: 'She looks at the pond with clear eyes. The fish are fake and swim in electronic circles [. . .] It's all a false enchantment' (227). In this saccharine artificial environment, its inhabitants breathe manufactured air and consume blandly processed food. Caledon is a metaphor for Caledonia, a traditional patriarchal nation that conjures images of romanticized Scotland. His dream becomes others' nightmare, as his megalomania 'filled him with a ruthlessness that turned his heart to stone' (194). Through Mara and Fox, Bertagna envisages a dismantling of Caledon/Caledonia's patriarchal binaries towards a more feminine androgynous balance, where Scottish society is relocated in an outward move towards a hybrid, supranational world of inclusion, where it can be *'Free at last!'*, for 'We all have to open our eyes now and look beyond this godforsaken place at the edge of the Earth' (9). Fox, as an example of Scotland's new androgyny, describes himself as *'a child of the world'* (*Exodus* 330). It is clear, then, that Mara's exodus cannot conclude in New Mungo, for 'the New World was to be only for what it judged to be the best of human beings [. . .] Everyone else was regarded as an alien, an outcast [. . .] instead of reaching a hand outwards to help the survivors of the floods, all the imagination and energy of the citizens of the New World turned inward' (196). Instead she must endeavour to relocate her people, a diverse alien populace, to a climate receptive to starting a new story of Scotland that transcends Caledon's parochial borders. Bertagna chooses Greenland as this new place, whose name, we're told, translates as 'The land of the people', suggesting a democratic hope that it 'Could [. . .] be the key to their future' (145). Though an ordinary girl, Mara shakes the foundations of New Mungo, significantly, from below and struggles to rebuild a nation of equality.

She utilizes the imaginary space provided by fiction in order to envisage alternative futures within a fluid seascape that transcends national divisions and favours, instead, nomadic relocation to an Arctic land of the people. *Exodus* and *Zenith* dislocate regional borders to envisage nomadic supranational citizens who fluidly chart a feminine route through the interstices of heteropatriarchy's cultural discourse. Mara is drawn to Greenland because of the information she acquires from a fragment of a book about

> *a mobile people who inhabit the huge, mountainous boreal forests of the Arctic Circle, one of the emptiest, most forgotten places on Earth. They have not devastated the natural world around them as so-called civilized societies have, but have co-existed in fine balance with the land and its animals for thousands of* [. . .] The rest of the paper fragment is torn. (154)

Nomadically shifting to the Arctic, described in *Exodus* as '*one of the emptiest, most forgotten places on Earth*', offers spatial malleability to recreate anew. In such an uncharted feminine wilderness, the fixed map of phallogocentric meaning dissipates, allowing Other identities to emerge. Bertagna says, 'My imagination is just drawn there. I know a lot of writers explore there I suppose because it's an unexplored place. So it was somewhere for my imagination to roam [. . .] that imaginative space' (McCulloch 2007a: 82). Peter Davidson's *The Idea of North* (which Bertagna has read) associates this link between the geographical North and imaginative writers, seeing 'The idea of north as a place of purification, an escape from the limitations of civilization' (Davidson 2005: 21). Davidson points out that 'North is always a shifting idea, always relative' (Davidson 2005: 8) and Barry Lopez in *Arctic Dreams* argues that 'Part of the allure of the Arctic has always been the very imprecision of its borders' (Lopez 1999 [1986]: 282). Just as Mara is drawn to the notion of '*a mobile people*' who have loosened geographical ties in favour of a shifting home, the notion of the Arctic itself offers the allure of permeability and the emergence of newly imagined identities. Notice that Mara only reads a fragment of the book about these nomadic Arctic people because the rest of the page has been torn. The point is that, as the heroine of Bertagna's book(s), she must build upon the stories of a palimpsest past in order to write her own future. She is not authorized by the rigid scripts of the phallic Father of Caledon/Caledonia, but is free to roam away from this and create a new evolving story for her people.

One of the problems of Caledon's brave new sky-world is that it does not want to preserve a sense of its heritage but, instead, to erase its past as systematically as George Orwell's Oceania in *1984*. We are told 'The past is banished. It's been deleted. All everyone ever thinks of is here and now' (Bertagna 2003 [2002]: 262). Devoid of the story of their traditions, the citizens of New Mungo are negated of a communal story upon which to found the keystone of their future. Bertagna's message is that 'It's about infecting the present with the past and – with luck – changing the future' (Bertagna 2003 [2002]: 284) because, without learning from one's mistakes and moving beyond patriarchy's will to power and resultant appetite for destruction, the premise is that the cycle of destruction will blindly perpetuate itself. Her remedy is to incorporate the lessons of its past into its present in order to reposition Scotland's future in a plethora of supranational narratives. As her heroine, Mara herself is a fusion of past, present and future, given that she, we are told 'is the image of Thenew' (Bertagna 2003 [2002]: 116), who is the mother of St. Mungo, the Patron Saint of Glasgow but, unlike Thenew, Mara gives birth not to a boy, but a girl as the future generation's leader.

In order to build a future of diverse citizens, Mara's people are a multiplicity of identities, and her daughter, Lily, symbolizes a peaceful hybrid fusion of the old world (as her mother, Mara, lost her Scottish island home to global warming), and the new world (her father, Fox, is a freedom-fighter yet a product of New Mungo). Several travellers to this new 'land of the people' ponder their new citizenship, with questions such as, 'So who am I? What am I now?' (Bertagna 2007: 317). In order to reach their new settlement, Mara and her people must emerge from a cave, which is closely associated with a birth, for 'The tunnel presses in on all sides [. . .] She begins to slide her body around the curve of the bend, to push herself forward limb by limb [. . .] Gasping and sweating [. . .] They have made it through!' (Bertagna 2007: 268). Being metaphorically reborn from the birth canal of Mother Earth allows them to start afresh, yet armed with the knowledge of their forefathers' mistakes. But charting the rebirth of a nation will include the birth pangs of uncertainty and struggle, as Mara's citizens endure the hardships of writing their own futures. Part of the rebirth of the nation involves redressing the gender balance – when she is in the library of a submerged Glasgow University, Mara notices a distinct lack of women's names in the names of great thinkers who shaped the world, what she refers to as 'the missing women in the mosaic of creation' (Bertagna 2003 [2002]: 175) and recognizes that her own dream will form part of a new Scottish story. Beyond a gender shortfall, Bertagna recognizes that social class also creates a gap in this historical narrative, for 'With a stab of pain, Mara thinks of her father [. . .] and all the unknown, ordinary men who farmed the land [. . .] But still, there are no women at all' (Bertagna 2003 [2002]: 175). This reflects the political climate, where 'There is a strong consensus that the Scottish Parliament must be a different type of legislature, one which is accessible to women and others traditionally excluded from formal arenas of politics' (Brown et al. 1998: 197).

Having the benefit of mobility, Mara's people liberate themselves from an imposed national identity, seeing themselves as aliens on a new planet, while simultaneously nurturing the positive roots of their homeland. Given the nomadism of Mara's people, Bertagna's fiction is equally fluid in its open-endedness, as it refuses to be pinned down. She says, 'If things aren't tied up then there's energy there' (McCulloch 2007a: 95). In *Zenith* these travellers remind us that

> 'We're still living our story [. . .] We don't know how it will end [. . .] Mara saved us and we're not Treenesters trapped in the netherworld any more. You', he speaks to the refugees from the boat camp, 'are not shut out of the world, dying outside the city wall. And you're not ratkins any more [. . .] We are all people now. People of the free world on the way to our home'. (Bertagna 2007: 94–5)

Bertagna herself notes 'Scotland is in transition, I suppose that must inform your imagination [. . .] I am writing about characters who are all in transition' (McCulloch 2007a: 95). For children's literature it implies that there are new frontiers and challenges ahead, that the child hero/heroine will not always have a safe journey, that adults may create dangers rather than security, and the only way forward is to denounce patriarchal restrictions on gender and nation while creating dynamic identities.

READING

Lucie Armitt, *Theorising the Fantastic* (1996).
Joseph Bristow, *Empire Boys* (1991).

Peter Hunt (ed.), *Understanding Children's Literature* (2005).

Peter Hunt and Millicent Lenz, *Alternative Worlds in Fantasy Fiction* (2001).

Linda M. Shires, 'Fantasy, Nonsense, Parody, and the Status of the Real: The Example of Carroll', *Victorian Poetry*, 26:3, Autumn 1988.

Fiona McCulloch, *The Fictional Role of Childhood in Victorian and Early Twentieth-Century Children's Literature* (2004).

Fiona McCulloch, '"A New Home in the World": Scottish Devolution, Nomadic Writing, and Supranational Citizenship in Julie Bertagna's *Exodus and Zenith*', *Ariel*, 38:4, Oct. 07, 69–96.

Heather Montgomery and Nicola J. Watson, *Children's Literature* (2009).

Roni Natov, *The Poetics of Childhood* (2006 [2003]).

Kimberley Reynolds, *Girls Only?* (1990).

Jacqueline Rose, *The Case of Peter Pan* (1994 [1984]).

David Rudd, *The Routledge Companion to Children's Literature* (2010).

Margaret and Michael Rustin, *Narratives of Love and Loss* (2001).

Rosemary Jackson, *Fantasy: The Literature of Subversion* (1998 [1981]).

RESEARCH

In what ways does Carroll make use of nonsense in *Alice*?

Give examples of orality and explain their use.

To what extent are the *Alice* books an exploration of identity?

Describe the island and how far it might be offering a critique of colonialism in Stevenson's *Treasure Island*.

Explore the narrative structure and explain how this complicates innocence in children's literature.

In what ways is Silver 'playing double'? Give specific examples from the text.

To what extent does Baum's *The Wonderful Wizard of Oz* offer a space in which the cultural Other can be heard?

Explore the motif of the journey and explain its significance.

In what ways has 'home' been altered by the ending of Baum's novel?

What is the relationship between childhood and nature in Burnett's *The Secret Garden*?

Explore the Gothic elements in the text and explain their function.

How satisfactory do you find the ending? Give reasons.

Describe the different settings in Lewis's *The Lion, The Witch and the Wardrobe* and explain their significance.

How are gender roles explored?

Jackson says that 'Fantasy in literature deals so blatantly and repeatedly with unconscious material that it seems rather absurd to try to understand its significance without some reference to psychoanalysis and psychoanalytic readings of texts' (Jackson 1981: 6). To what extent can Lewis's text (or, indeed, any of the fantasy discussed) be read as an exploration of the psyche?

Explore the differences and similarities between Harry and Voldemort in Rowling's series.

How significant is setting? Give some examples and explain their function.

Explore the representation of gender in Rowling's series.

Describe Lyra and the ways in which she is a strong heroine in Pullman's trilogy.

How are themes of good and evil explored?

What is Dust? Explain its significance.

What challenges face Mara in Bertagna's series and how does she overcome them?

How significant is the theme of the journey and home?

To what extent is Bertagna's story concerned with nation and how far does it explore cosmopolitan issues?

CHAPTER FOUR

CRITICAL CONTEXTS

EARLY CRITICS

John Rowe Townsend's *Written for Children* (1965) provides a socio-historical response to the continuum of children's literature as well as a critical engagement with genres like the school story and the structures of fantasy and realism. It still offers an insightful introduction to the subject, albeit overtaken by historical events and theoretical developments. Also key in early commentaries upon children's literature were Peter and Iona Opie. Their studies included *The Oxford Dictionary of Nursery Rhymes* (1951) and *The Lore and Language of Schoolchildren* (1959). Generally, however, the academic study of children's literature was woefully neglected, with it being regarded as a somewhat Cinderella subject unworthy of serious highbrow academic critique. The knock-on effect of this was that the subject was not studied at university level until well into the twentieth century and has only recently become a popular pursuit in recent years. The rise of literary theory has had a significant impact on the study of children's literature: like hitherto marginalized areas, such as women's writing or lesbian and gay literature, children's fiction has been decentred and recentred in order to consider its critical and cultural merits.

Given its lack of academic support, it is perhaps unsurprising that it tended to be regarded with hostility by many male academics and rendered more suitable for women to dabble in. So, too, has the actual creative writing craft of fiction for children generally been more popular with female than male authors. In addition, the sense of where the subject actually belongs has been a source of ongoing debate, with academics disagreeing over whether it should be housed in educational studies as a pedagogical aspect of childhood development or whether it is more comfortable in English studies, given that its composition is the literary text. While these debates continue, it cannot be ignored that children's literature continues to be extremely popular with the public, big business for publishers, financially lucrative for some authors and is increasingly popular in Higher Education both at undergraduate and postgraduate levels. Responding to much of this is the steadily increasing number of academics who specialize and publish in the area, including Jacqueline Rose, Peter Hunt, Kimberley Reynolds, Fiona McCulloch, Roderick McGillis, M.O. Grenby, David Rudd, Joseph Bristow, John Stephens, Perry Nodelman, Roni Natov, Jack Zipes and Marina Warner, with the likes of Gilles Deleuze and Hélène Cixous contributing to discussions of Lewis Carroll's *Alice* books.

SIGNIFICANT CRITICISM

Thanks to literary theory, children's literature is one of several marginalized fields (including, for instance, women's writing, queer theory, and postcolonialism) that has acquired recent academic interest. Because of the diversity of literary and cultural theory upon which critics draw, the lens of children's literary criticism is richly diverse and views its subject through many kaleidoscopic approaches ranging from poststructural deconstruction of texts to feminist theoretical readings.

Jacqueline Rose's *The Case of Peter Pan; or the Impossibility of Children's* Fiction (1984) is a seminal study in the children's literature critical canon, itself becoming a bestseller, with a revised edition published in 1994. A pivotal text in the theoretical approach to the subject, Rose employs Freudian theory to argue that fiction written for children is largely impossible, given its unstable and unequal relationship between adult author and child reader. She applies her complex and sophisticated analysis to J.M. Barrie's *Peter Pan* as the focal case of her argument. The desire to maintain childhood innocence according to Rose coincides with a mission within the rubric of children's literature to return language to a supposed prelapsarian state, before one has been polluted by social influences. Responding to Jean-Jacques Rousseau and John Locke, she contests that language within children's fiction is reduced to its most transparent, enabling the child to have an immediate and clear relation to the material world described. As such, it is privileges realism, while metaphorical language is avoided lest its lack of straightforward literal meaning corrupt the truthfulness of the narrative. As John Stephens notes in *Language and Ideology in Children's Fiction*:

> A book "based on a true story" is inherently preferable to a book which is a mere fiction; language which evokes 'the real world' is preferable to language which doesn't [. . .] its effect is to imply a one-to-one relationship between objects and their representation, and hence to mask the processes of textual production of meaning: representation becomes equated with "truth".
> (Stephens 1992: 4)

Rose goes on to argue that this drive towards unadulterated language stems from the childhood discourse that regards the child as uncorrupted and pure: adult culture strives to tap into this dual purity, thereby enabling a restoration through childhood and its literary rubric. Consequently, innocence of the child and of the word reinforce and perpetuate each other within children's fiction, acting as a medium to produce linguistic purity and represent the childhood ideal. An ideal of course reminds us that such a childhood space is ultimately empty until filled with discourse.

Rose contests that it is this Rousseauist spin on childhood which has shaped children's literature from the Romantic period right up to our contemporary society, where there is a continual association between purity of child and purity of literary form. While this may well be the cultural demand or intention for children's literature, nevertheless such an ideal form is not met and, indeed, is often subverted to open up a debate in respect to contemporaneous discourses of childhood. Moreover, Rose's deployment of J.M. Barrie's *Peter Pan* and its origins as an adult novel, *The Little White Bird*, as a metafictional (when a text is aware of its own artifice) commentary upon children's fiction, cannot be regarded as a story best suited to examining literary tensions within that genre precisely *because* it is derived from an adult text. To claim that Barrie's novel is ideal due to its position of observing and commenting upon children's literature as initially an adult text surely does a grave injustice to the plethora of texts available written specifically as children's books. Children's fiction, while it may appear to be "innocent", often contains layered complexities that engage with dominant discourses rather than merely reflects them. These texts problematize transparent realism by manipulating a textual lens that actively distorts the representation of childhood and highlights the fictionalized mythical status of the child subject within adult discourse.

Regarding specifically the medium of children's literature, Rose equates this cultural turn towards innocence as manifesting itself textually to provide closure at the end of a story, where transparent realism maintains that meaning is enclosed and contained within its literary covers. Whilst this may indeed be a cultural desire, children's fiction resists straightforward interpretation, instead exposing self-conscious gaps, ambiguities, ironies and often subversive engagement with contemporaneous ideologies. As Perry Nodelman confirms:

> Rose ignores the ambiguity that underlies the apparent simplicity of most good children's books, for she seems to be determined to read children's books in terms of the quite limited and often wrongheaded assertions that critics and authors make about them [. . .] Far too many writers and critics want children's fiction to represent all that is true and good in both life and literature, as opposed to the supposed sickness and decadence and chaos of contemporary life and of all other modern fiction. The trouble with Rose's argument is that she actually *believes* these ridiculous comments that writers and critics make about children's books. In doing so, she misses most of what is interesting about children's fiction. (Nodelman 1985: 99)

Through the preceding chapters I hope to have exposed some of these literary ambiguities and invited a consideration 'of what is most interesting' about the texts under discussion.

Such instances of a cultural desire to reinforce the parameters of childhood innocence are prevalent within moments of late twentieth-century crisis and tended to parallel Victorian discourses upon childhood and the requirement for its literary rubric to offer purity of form and content, and also echo the cultural privileging of the nuclear family. Such constructions exist to reassure adult society at the denial of the individual child. Sigmund Freud challenged dominant representations in his study of childhood sexuality, arguing that the child is not innocent but bisexual and polymorphously perverse, meaning that it has multiple erogenous zones that give it pleasure including, for instance, the mouth during the oral stage of development. Such oral pleasure, for instance, is removed when the child is "civilized" by social instruction (Freud 1991 [1905]). According to Rose, it serves adult culture to deny the existence of childhood sexuality and promote discourses of purity because Freud identified childhood sexual perversion, which is threatening to adult identity and society. As an Other, such perversion must be suppressed and denied until the maturity of adulthood instils a normative sexuality, thus distancing the centralized norm from such polymorphous deviance. Freud tends to take a conservative reactionary stance in identifying any remnants of perversion in adulthood and blindly grouping them in the same prejudiced category of other, such as homosexuality or paedophilia (even contemporary society can be guilty of misrepresenting these two very distinct groups by homogenizing them). However, Rose also notes that Freud raises the vital point that childhood is not an alien form from which we metamorphose into the altogether different species of adulthood, but remains integral to our adult identity. Any sexual perversity or desires are repressed from the conscious mind and secured in our unconscious, only to emerge in parapraxes, such as slips of the tongue, puns and, importantly, imaginative language. Pierre Macherey (1978) discusses the literary unconscious which exposes itself through gaps and silences that decentre the text. Children's literature as a literary form is riddled with gaps, silences and fissures that threaten its apparent prelapsarian transparency with dark unconscious undercurrents and a postlapsarian author. In *A Theory of Literary Production* (1978), Macherey refers to the importance of a literary unconscious exposed through gaps and silences which serve to decentre the text.

Kimberley Reynolds is an important children's literature theorist, responsible for a considerable output of critical material, including *Girls Only? Gender and Popular Children's Fiction in Britain, 1880–1910* (1990), *Children's Literature in the 1890s and the 1990s* (1994), [co-edited with Gillian Avery] *Representations of Childhood Death* (2000), [co-written with Geraldine Brennan and Kevin McCarron] *Frightening Fiction* (2001) *Modern Children's Literature: An Introduction* (2005), *Radical Children's Literature: Future Visions and Aesthetic Transformations in Juvenile Fiction* (2007). Reynolds reads with a socio-historical as well as psychofeminist slant, considering the impact on the literature studied of literary and cultural influences such as the *fin de siècle* both at the close of the nineteenth and twentieth centuries, or the manifestations of gender constructions in fiction for children. Regarding the nineteenth century as a time when the child and its literature becomes sentimentalized, she also demonstrates the impact of *fin de siècle* anxieties on British masculinity, with an emphasis on hyper-manliness and domestic femininity as the ideal states for the maintenance of the nation's empire. Conventionally regarded as a 'safe-house' (Reynolds 1994: 24), children's literature is actually filled with undercurrents of sexual tensions and eroticism emanating from its authors, particularly in the late Victorian era. By comparison, Reynolds regards post-war children's fiction as being less prone to stem from the (often male) author's psychosexual anxieties and more concerned with a collective consciousness regarding 'the present state of civilization' and the cultural pressures facing childhood 'as part of the process of growing up: fear of separation, loss, sexuality, death, anger, and so on' (Reynolds 1994: 41).

In terms of gender, Reynolds argues that Victorian Britain generates a significantly wider gap between boys and girls in the deliberate production of ideological reading material for boys that laid great emphasis upon lack of emotions and instead focused upon 'a predictable, knowable world by supplying information and answers and suppressing problematic personal questions' (Reynolds 1990: 37). The rise of the boy's adventure tale, then, is hardly surprising in this period, with its emphasis on action, derring-do, sea quests, shipwrecks, jingoism and lack of active female characters. Examples include Captain Marryat's *Mr Midshipman Easy* (1836) and *Masterman Ready* (1841–42), Charles Kingsley's *Westward Ho!* (1855), R.M. Ballantyne's *The Coral Island* (1858) and Robert Louis Stevenson's *Treasure Island* (1883). At the same time, a hierarchical binary opposition ensured that 'masculinity became more valued and more elusive than ever before and this inevitably resulted in a devaluation of femininity' (Reynolds 1990: 40). Instead of the largely outdoor world pursuits of boy's adventure stories, literature for girls became polarized around the static confines of the home and domestic interests and included 'examining relationships and internal states' (Reynolds 1990: 43). While the boy was being prepared for a life at the outer regions of Britain's vast empire, the girl was being raised as the next generation of maternal nurturers, the Angel-in-the-House whose life mission was self-sacrifice and passive compliance to masculine demands. Such writers included Evelyn Everett-Green, L.T. Meade, Louisa May Alcott and Susan Coolidge. But, of course, many girls also read books intended for boys and this raises questions about how far girls internalized passive roles and to what extent they identified with active male heroes.

Peter Hunt continues to be a prolific academic critic in the field of children's literature. *Literature for Children: Contemporary Criticism* (1992) brings together several theoretical interpretations of a variety of children's texts from an array of critics. For instance, Peter Hollindale outlines the ideological implications of children's literature, arguing that it 'is present in a children's book in three main ways' (Hunt 1992: 27) which are identified as: 'the explicit social, political or moral beliefs of the individual writer, and his wish to recommend them to children through the story' (Hunt 1992: 27), 'the individual writer's unexamined assumptions' (Hunt 1992: 30) and, finally, the text itself insofar as 'we must think in terms which include but also transcend the idea of individual authorship' since 'ideology is inseparable from language' (Hunt 1992: 32–3). In his introduction Hunt points out that 'the emergence of children's literature' can be compared with 'other "new" literatures [national, ethnic, feminist, post-colonial]' (Hunt 1992: 2), continuing that it is 'fortunate that the growth of children's literature studies has coincided with the burgeoning of literary theory', given theory's propensity to

> breakdown [. . .] the established literary canon and with it the dominance of literary studies in the humanities; the acceptance of reader response and deconstruction; a questioning of the power structures of western culture; the development of new readings of history and literature (such as feminist or post-colonial), and the acceptance of new readings and new literatures as equal but different. (Hunt 1992: 10)

With that in mind this book offers a plethora of readings, including mention of metafiction, postmodernism and new historicism.

In *An Introduction to Children's Literature* (1994), Hunt provides an overview of the history and culture of children's literature, tracing its evolutionary journey from eighteenth century (though identifying that children did read prior to this) through to the late twentieth century. As well as this, he offers a discussion of the position that children's literature occupies in the field of literature generally insofar as it has been regarded as peripheral to serious literary works, while it has also been marginalized within academic study . 'Consequently', observes Hunt, 'children's books do not fit easily into the patriarchal world of literary/cultural values. They are [. . .] primarily the domain of women writers (and, latterly, women educators), just as children are: in that literary hierarchy they are necessarily at the bottom of the heap' (Hunt 1994: 6–7). He continues, 'It hardly comes as a surprise to find that among specialist children's literature teachers at colleges in the United States, for example, "about 92% are women; about 50% are assistant professors; about 40% are associate professors and only 5[%] are professors"' (Hunt 1994: 6–7). An obvious gender gap is distinguishable as well as a correlation between gender and economic impoverishment, just as children's literature has itself been the poor relation in the critical appreciation and evaluation of literature. His appraisal of the history of fairy tales as an area of children's literature that has been inherited from oral folk tales and that have been subject to numerous versions and rewritings as being 'only of interest to the specialist scholar' (Hunt 1994: 28) is problematic when he has only just lambasted academia for its failure to take the subject seriously. Commenting that such variations and revisions are unimportant 'to the child, to the real reader' (Hunt 1994: 28) simplifies the relationship between children's fiction and its reader in a reductive manner that inaccurately assumes that the text is never written in any manner that may address an adult reader. This seems to give rise to the naïve suggestion that any academic textual deconstruction would by unworthy or perhaps over reading since it would be done by someone unreal.

Nevertheless, a sound overarching discussion of children's literature offers a survey of its changing literary and cultural history, as well as indicating some recurrent themes, such as journeys, the debate between realism and fantasy as being appropriate vehicles and a consideration of the role of censorship. Hunt's most recent guide is *Children's Literature* (2001), which combines historical, biographical and critical interpretations of an array of writers and their works. While far-reaching in its capacity, Hunt's observations feel somewhat restrictive given the short nature of each chapter, which leaves little room for manoeuvrable depth. Hunt is prolific in this area, also publishing the self-explanatory *Children's Literature: An Illustrated History* (1995) and *Understanding Children's Literature*, Second Edition (2007 [2005]). In the latter, several contributors address debates concerning the construction of childhood, intertextuality and setting, offering a useful variety of theoretical positionings. Hunt's *Alternative Worlds in Fantasy Fiction* (2001), a guide co-authored with Millicent Lenz, considers fantasy within children's literature, offering a close analysis of three key writers of fantasy for children: Ursula Le Guin, Terry Pratchett and Philip Pullman. The discussion focuses upon main themes that arise in their works, as well as providing some biographical details.

Jack Zipes is best known for his work on fairy tales, placing them in a socio-historical context that charts their journey from oral folk tales heard by all generations to modern literary fairy tales aimed specifically at children. *Fairy Tales and the Art of Subversion: The Classical Genre for Children and the Process of Civilization* (1991 [1983]) challenges the assumption that such stories are timeless and universal, overturning this with a Marxist historicist approach that takes into account the ideological implications of a genre that sought to naturalize class and gender hegemonies, since 'The morality and ethics of a male-dominated Christian civil order had to become part and parcel of the literary fairy tale' (Zipes 1991 [1983]: 9). As such 'They are historical prescriptions, internalized, potent, explosive, and we acknowledge the power they hold over our lives by mystifying them' (Zipes 1991 [1983]: 11). In the nineteenth century revival of the fairy tale by Victorian writers like George MacDonald, Oscar Wilde and L. Frank Baum, Zipes charts the potential subversion of their works in challenging earlier ideological tales. For them, 'No longer was the fairy tale to be like the mirror, mirror on the wall reflecting the cosmetic bourgeois standards of beauty and virtue which appeared to be unadulterated and pure' (Zipes 1991 [1983]: 99). Rather, 'The fairy tale and the mirror cracked into sharp-edged, radical parts by the end of the nineteenth century' (Zipes 1991 [1983]: 99).

In *Don't Bet on the Prince: Contemporary Feminist Fairy Tales in North America and England* (1989 [1986]), he continues the theme of subversive fairy tales by introducing a collection of feminist tales that seek to shatter the mirror of the gender ideal. In his introduction Zipes discusses why such a collection is deemed necessary as a

challenge to social conventions that are internalized and natural-
ized in our formative years through the affect of traditional tales,
for 'It is not by coincidence that numerous feminist critics, women
and men, feel that the fairy tales of their childhood stamp their
present actions and behaviour in reality' (Zipes 1986: 9). What is
learned in childhood, then, is carried with us into the adult world
where the cycle of gender dichotomies is perpetuated without
question. As an antidote to such cultural poisoning, Zipes's collection offers a bite of an altogether more satisfying apple that
'explore new possibilities for gender arrangement' (Zipes 1986: 26).
Shaping and being shaped by socio-historical shifts, 'How we have
arranged ourselves, our bodies and psyches, in society has been
recorded and passed down through fairy tales for many centuries,
and the contemporary feminist tales indicate that something radical is occurring in Western society to change our social and political relations' (Zipes 1986: 26).

Sticks and Stones (2002 [2001]) traces what Zipes refers to as the
'troublesome success' of children's literature up until Rowling's
Harry Potter, arguing that 'Phenomena such as the Harry Potter
books are driven by commodity consumption' (Zipes 2001: 172).
This is symptomatic of the wider rubric of children's literature since
'the conditions under which literature for the young is produced
and received have been transformed through institutional changes
of education, shifts in family relations, the rise of corporate con-
glomerates controlling the mass media, and the market demands'
(Zipes 2001: 172). Ideologically ensnared within social demands,
Zipes contests that Rowling's books 'are ordinary and yet have
become extraordinary' (Zipes 2001: 174) because of commodity
appeal. 'They are easy and delightful to read' he argues, 'carefully
manicured and packaged, and they sell extraordinarily well precisely because they are so cute and ordinary' (Zipes 2001: 175).

JAMES R. KINCAID, JOHN STEPHENS, PERRY NODELMAN, DAVID RUDD AND HUGH CUNNINGHAM

Kincaid's *Child-Loving* (1992) controversially posits that there is
something unwholesome about the adult cultural drive to preserve
childhood innocence, combining a socio-historical discussion of
Victorian society with an examination of Barrie's *Peter Pan* and

Carroll's *Alice*. He considers the ideological power imbalance child/ adult relations, noting that

> we live under the assumption that children are especially privileged and that our entire culture is 'child-centred', but the 'romantic mythology' encrusting childhood is very much like that used for racial and gender power-moves: 'children', 'coloreds', and women are all depicted as naturally carefree, fortunate to be unsuited to the burdens of autonomy and decision-making, and better off protected by those in control. (Kincaid1992: 64)

Demonizing the paedophile as a corrupter of childhood, he argues that mainstream society deflects the problematic desire that exists for all adult culture, given that it imposes an ideological matrix of childhood upon children. Childhood is, then, culturally determined, since 'the "child" is nothing more than what it is considered to be, nothing in itself at all' (Kincaid 1992: 90). Flouting stereotypes, he notes that 'in one important study, most of the subjects were not old; most did not abuse drugs or alcohol [. . .] and none were homosexuals' (Kincaid 1992: 187–8), while 'the most respected empirical studies reluctantly admit that adult offenders against boys are 'almost uniformly heterosexual and not homosexual' (Kincaid 1992: 191).

Stephens's *Language and Ideology in Children's Fiction* (1992) develops the link between power and children's fiction, noting that it is 'through language that literature seeks to define the relationship between child and culture' (Stephens 1992: 5). Power structures can either be overt pedagogical lessons or covertly introduced, for, 'Fiction presents a special context for the operation of ideologies, because narrative texts are highly organized and structured discourses whose conventions may either be used to express deliberate advocacy of social practices or may encode social practices implicitly. They may do both', while 'A text may overtly advocate one ideology while implicitly inscribing one or more other ideologies' (Stephens 1992: 43). Nodelman counters Rose's view that innocence dominates children's texts, insisting that the books are full of complex meaning, while 'Rose ignores the ambiguity that underlies the apparent simplicity of most good children's books, for she seems to be determined to read children's books in terms of the quite limited and often wrongheaded assertions that critics and authors make about them' (Nodelman 1985: 99). Most recently, he considers the 'hidden adult' influencing children's fiction, be it the author, parent, teacher or wider culture. 'Whether or not child readers do match how adults think about them, the children in the phrase "children's literature" are most usefully understood as the child reader that writers, responding to the assumptions of adult purchasers, imagine and imply in their works' (Nodelman 2008: 5).

Rudd's *Enid Blyton and the Mystery of Children's Literature* (2000) offers an astute study of Blyton's oeuvre within the wider tenets of children's literature, covering theoretically sophisticated commentary with a sound close analysis of motifs in several of her books, such as the mystery of secret passages. His theoretical positioning extends to a discussion of the construction of childhood and the literary representation of this, where the child itself exists as a hybrid state between, 'arguing that the child is necessarily both constructed and constructive, and that this hybrid border country is worthy of exploration' (Hunt, Second Edition 2007 [2005]: 25). Cunningham is a cultural historian of childhood who charts the ways in which childhood evolves depending on its historical and social circumstances. So, the movement towards innocence is equated with a social change in employment laws: 'if adults were burdened with responsibilities, children should be carefree. If adults worked, children should not work' but were 'entitled to contact with nature' (Cunningham 1996 [1995]: 160). This also coincided with a focus upon the child within the nuclear family, for 'by the middle of the twentieth century the death of a baby was something which few parents would experience [. . .] and consequently the notion of family planning could take on new meaning' (Cunningham 1996 [1995]: 165). Ultimately, he argues, 'mostly what we hear are adults imagining childhood, inventing it, in order to make sense of their world. Children have to live with the consequences' (Cunningham 2006: 12).

It is worth thinking about some theoretical perspectives of Fantasy literature and to relate that specifically to children's fantasy literature. Tzvetan Todorov's *The Fantastic* (1975 [1970]) provides a structural approach for defining a poetics of the fantastic as a particular fictional genre. The fantastic, he argues, exists as a point between the uncanny and the marvellous. He says of the fantastic that it is 'located on the frontier of two genres, the marvelous and the uncanny, rather than to be an autonomous genre'

(Todorov 1970: 41). He defines the uncanny as the 'supernatural explained' and the marvellous as the 'supernatural accepted'. So an uncanny tale would seek to discover and thereby disclose to the reader a rational explanation for events which appear to be super-natural – in this way the story is neatly contained and closure is affected (e.g., the gothic novels of Ann Radcliffe). The marvellous, on the other hand, is that which defies explanation and remains in the realm of the possibly supernatural, such as the fairy tale or sci-ence fiction. Fantasy literature, then, exists at a point between two literary worlds and therefore, by this very implication, it becomes in itself a genre that cannot be defined or ultimately pinned down – in essence it is negated. Fantasy takes the identifiable real world and adds a twist and the reader is left to negotiate whether its super-natural impulse can be reduced to logical interpretation or remain forever elusive. Todorov says

> The fantastic occupies the duration of this uncertainty. Once we choose one answer or the other, we leave the fantastic for a neigh-boring genre, the uncanny or the marvelous. The fantastic is that hesitation experienced by a person who knows only the laws of nature, confronting an apparently supernatural event. (Todorov 1970: 25)

He argues that 'The fantastic' exists only during a hesitant moment which is 'common to reader and character, who must decide whether or not what they perceive derives from "reality" as it exists in the common opinion. At the story's end, the reader makes a decision even if the character does not; he opts for one solution or the other, and thereby emerges from the fantastic' (Todorov 1970: 41). If the reader decides that the fantastic moment can be explained ration-ally 'we say that the work belongs to another genre: the uncanny' (Todorov1970: 41). However, if the experience exists outside of rational familiarity 'we enter the genre of the marvellous' (Todorov 1970: 41). Because of its temporality, 'The fantastic therefore leads a life full of dangers, and may evaporate at any moment' (Todorov 1970: 41).

Rosemary Jackson's *Fantasy: the Literature of Subversion* (1998 [1981]) builds upon yet criticizes Todorov's model by insisting that his lack of consideration of psychoanalytic or socio-historical influ-ences upon fantasy literature leave it locked in an ahistorical time

warp and ignores the crucial ideological influences upon any literary work. She suggests that from the late eighteenth century a shift
occurs from the marvellous to the uncanny, as society experiences a
cultural transition from religious mysticism towards profanity and
scientific thought. Fantasy exists as the space between which serves
to disrupt or subvert the dominant nineteenth century literary
mode of realism, which sought to mimetically reflect the outside
world within the novel form. As society became increasingly industrialized, Jackson argues, fantasy served as a critique of entrepre-
neurial capitalism and its cultural effects (e.g., Charles Kingsley's
The Water-Babies [1863] considers the environmental implications
of industrial waste). The ultimate revolutionary aspect of fantasy's
subversive potential is questioned, however, as often the dominant
cultural discourses within which each particular text is produced,
can be reasserted and reconfirmed. What is interesting, though,
is the textual eruption, albeit temporally, which occurs within the
framework of realist truth. Thus, Jackson writes that 'fantastic literature points to or suggests the basis upon which cultural order
rests', as it spatially allows, briefly, the 'illegality' of 'that which
lies outside the law, that which is outside dominant value systems'
(Jackson 1981: 4). For Jackson, 'The fantastic traces the unsaid and
the unseen of culture: that which has been silenced, made invisible,
covered over and made "absent"' (Jackson 1981: 4). In other words,
fantasy considers the cultural Other. Rather than perceiving fantasy
as a genre, Jackson suggests that 'fantasy is a literary mode from
which a number of related genres emerge. Fantasy provides a range
of possibilities out of which various combinations produce different
kinds of fiction in different historical situations' (Jackson 1981: 7).
This definition of a multi-faceted fictional form might well be useful in considering children's literature as forming one of the spokes
under the diverse umbrella of fantasy literature. Other branches of
fantasy include the gothic novel, the horror novel, the ghost story,
or science fiction to name a few. Considering Jackson's discussion
of fantasy as a subversive exploration of cultural otherness, such
literature penned by those on society's margins, has the potential to
be a doubly subversive force. It is a literature which, to use Mikhail
Bakhtin's phrase, is dialogic. That is to say that fantasy is in dialogue or negotiation with the "real" and the stability of reality is
constantly challenged. The relationship between signifier and sig-
nified is disrupted and deferred, as the arbitrary nature of linguistic

sign and material truth is forever scrutinized. Often within fantasy the Other remains a shadowy presence which cannot be named or defined: a slippage occurs and this potentially undermines the authority and verisimilitude of patriarchal discourses as each text renegotiates and strives to move beyond social realism.

Lucie Armitt's *Theorising the Fantastic* (1996) extends Jackson's discussion to see fantasy as a particularly viable mode for women writers as it allows for the production of Other worlds where Other identities can be explored beyond the restrictive norms of realist writing. She says that 'Fantasy' is, as with all literature, 'fluid, constantly overspilling the very form it adopts, always looking, not so much for escapism but certainly to escape the constraints that critics [. . .] always and inevitably impose upon it' (Armitt 1996: 3). She continues, 'Now we can look at the fantastic as a form of writing which is about opening up subversive spaces within the mainstream rather than ghettoizing fantasy by encasing it within genres' (Armitt 1996: 3). David Gooderham discusses children's fantasy literature particularly, arguing that 'Fantasy is a metaphorical mode [. . .] *fantasy* is thus seen to describe not so much a collection of marvels which divert readers from ordinary human concerns, but a distinctive and fruitful way of speaking about just these concerns' (Gooderham 1995: 173). If fantasy is regarded, not as a way of escaping the world but as commenting upon society from a particular angle, then we need to consider how it functions in children's literature, which also comments upon its particular cultural period. For Ursula Le Guin, a prolific writer of adult and children's fantasy fiction, 'Fantasy is true, of course. It isn't factual, but it is true. Children know that. Adults know it too, and that is precisely why many of them are afraid of fantasy. They know that its truth challenges, even threatens, all that is false, all that is phoney, unnecessary, and trivial in the life they have let themselves be forced into living. They are afraid of dragons because they are afraid of freedom' (Le Guin (1980 [1979]: 44). According to Jacqueline Rose, children's literature has a necessity to be true yet fantasy can problematize this. Rousseau demanded that children should not be introduced to the language of metaphor because this would corrupt their purity and recommended they read *Robinson Crusoe* for its straightforward practicality. The response from the Christian Right in America to *Harry Potter* as promoting magic and evil might go some way to emphasizing the fear adult culture has in children reading works of fantasy. Critics like Jackson and Armitt have discussed the subversive potential of fantasy; in children's fantasy this becomes doubly dangerous as it might encourage the reader to critique social structures and norms. We have already seen how normality and identity are challenged in the fantasy realm of the *Alice* books.

CHAPTER FIVE

AFTERLIVES AND ADAPTATIONS

It is challenging to talk of afterlives when children's literature is burgeoning and ranges from picture books to young-adult cross-over fiction. Many classic texts have been revived through various mediums, including celluloid: for instance, Carroll's logic in the *Alice* books continues to influence contemporary culture. Andy and Lana Wachowski's *The Matrix* (1999) intertextualizes it when Neo is told to follow the white rabbit and is offered a choice of pills to ingest (just as Alice eats and drinks). The film picks up on the tension between reality and dream considered by Carroll when what is regarded to be real is revealed to be nothing more than a virtual reality constructed by a computer mainframe into which individuals are plugged.

Nicholas Wright has adapted Pullman's *His Dark Materials* into a theatre production that premiered in London in 2003. To date, the first part of the trilogy has been adapted for cinema in Chris Weitz's *The Golden Compass* (2007). There have been several cinematic adaptations of texts, including Agnieszka Holland's (dir) *The Secret Garden* (1993), Victor Fleming's *The Wizard of Oz* (1939), John Hough's *Treasure Island* (1972), Jack Gold's *Little Lord Fauntleroy* (1980), Ivan Popov's Russian version of *Little Lord Fauntleroy* (2003), Brian Henson's *Muppet Treasure Island* (1996), Gillian Armstrong's *Little Women* (1994), and Alfonso Cuaron's *A Little Princess* (1995). Warner Bros bought the film rights of *Harry Potter*, so far producing Chris Columbus's *Harry Potter and the Philosopher's Stone* (2000) and *Chamber of Secrets* (2002), Alfonso Cuaron's *Prisoner of Azkaban* (2004), Mike Newell's *Goblet of Fire* (2005), David Yates's *Order of the Phoenix* (2007) and *Half-Blood Prince* (2009). David Yates directed *Deathly Hallows*, which is in two parts, released in 2010 and 2011. Like many children's books, *Harry Potter* has spawned an emporium of board games, figurines and interactive multimedia games. Focusing on the life of Barrie as well as his work is Marc Forster's *Finding Neverland* (2004). Itself an adapted afterlife of Barrie's adult novel *The Little White Bird*, *Peter Pan* has been resurrected by Geraldine McCaughrean *Peter Pan in Scarlet* (2006), while Barrie's dream setting was reawakened to the controversy of Michael Jackson's ranch, Neverland. C.S. Lewis's life was explored in Richard Attenborough's *Shadowlands* (1993). As well as radio and stage adaptations, an adaption of Lewis's fiction was the BBC's 1988–90 four-part television series *The Chronicles of Narnia*, while Andrew Adamson adapted Lewis for the cinema with *The Chronicles of Narnia: The Lion, the Witch and the Wardrobe* (2005) and *Prince Caspian* (2008). Michael Apted's *Voyage of the Dawn Treader* is due for release in 2010.

Children's literature in its many variants continues to be big business and shows no signs of abating its commercial success in books, ebooks, toys, games, multimedia and cinema. Its success, however, extends beyond the monetary gain recognized by Robert Louis Stevenson when he wrote *Treasure Island*; it appeals to all sections of society from the very young to adults and continues to develop its interest for both students and academics in universities.

READING

Kristine Ohrem Bakke, *A Muggle's Study of Harry Potter's Magical World: J.K. Rowling's Literature Texts and Chris Columbus' Film Adaptations* (2010).

Dennis Butts (ed.), *Stories and Society: Children's Literature in its Social Context* (1992).

Mike Cadden, 'Home Is a Matter of Blood, Time, and Genre: Essentialism in Burnett and McKinley', *Ariel*, 28:1, Jan. 1997, 53–67.

Helene Cixous, 'Introduction to Lewis Carroll's *Through the Looking-Glass* and *The Hunting of the Snark* (1982), 231–51.

Nigel Hand, 'Anxieties of Authorship in the *Alice* Books; or, "Sentence First – Verdict Afterwards": The Trial of Lewis Carroll' in Broadbent et al. (eds) (1994), *Researching Children's Literature – A Coming of Age?* 36–43.

Margery Hourihan, *Deconstructing the Hero: Literary Theory and Children's Literature* (1997).

Thomas Leitch, *Film Adaptation and Its Discontents* (2007).

Fiona McCulloch, '"Playing Double": Performing Childhood in *Treasure Island*', *Scottish Studies Review*, 4:2, Autumn 2003, 66–81.

Jacqueline Rose, *The Case of Peter Pan; or the Impossibility of Children's Fiction* (1984).

Robert Stam et al., *Literature and Film: A Guide to the Theory and Practice of Film Adaptation* (2005).

John Stephens, *Language and Ideology in Children's Fiction* (1992).

RESEARCH

In what ways might children's literature benefit from using theoretical approaches, such as psychoanalytic theory?

Read John Stephens, Ch.1. To what extent is children's literature ideological?

Read Cadden's interpretation of *The Secret Garden*. What are the main points raised and how far do you agree with his argument?

Read Cixous's and Hand's essays on Carroll's work. What are the main arguments in both and how far do you agree with each of them?

To what extent does children's literature engage with and undermine discourses of childhood innocence?

To what extent are traditional children's stories problematic in their representations of gender and how far do contemporary texts redress this imbalance?

BIBLIOGRAPHY

Appiah, K.A. (2007 [2006]), *Cosmopolitanism: Ethics in a World of Strangers*. London and New York: Penguin.

Aries, P. (1973 [1962]), *Centuries of Childhood: A Social History of Family Life*. Harmondsworth: Penguin.

Armitt, L. (1996), *Theorising the Fantastic*. London: Arnold.

Avery, G., and Reynolds K. (eds) (2000), *Representations of Childhood Death*. London: Macmillan.

Bakke, K.O. (2010), *A Muggle's Study of Harry Potter's Magical World: J.K. Rowling's Literature Texts and Chris Columbus' Film Adaptations*. VDM Verlag Dr. Müller.

Barthes, R. (ed. and tr. by Stephen Heath) (1977), *Image Music Text*. London: Fontana Press.

Baum, L.F. (1992 [1900]), *The Wonderful Wizard of Oz*. London and New York: Everyman's Library.

Beck, U. (2007 [2004]), *Cosmopolitan Vision*. Cambridge: Polity Press.

Bell, E. (2004), *Questioning Scotland: Literature, Nationalism, Postmodernism*. Basingstoke: Palgrave Macmillan.

Bertagna, J. (2003 [2002]), *Exodus*. London: Pan Macmillan.

—. (2007), *Zenith*. London: Pan Macmillan.

Blackburn, W. (1983), 'Mirror in the Sea: *Treasure Island* and the Internalization of Juvenile Romance', *Children's Literature Association Quarterly*, 8:3.

Blake, W. (1994), *The Works of William Blake*. Ware: Wordsworth Editions.

Bloom, H. (ed.) (1987), *Modern Critical Views: Lewis Carroll*. New York and New Haven: Chelsea House Publishers.

Brennan, G., McCarron, K., and Reynolds, K. (2001), *Frightening Fiction*. London and New York: Continuum.

Bresnick, A. (1998), 'One Person's Eroticism is Another's Innocence' in *Times Literary Supplement*.

Bristow, J. (1991), *Empire Boys: Adventures in a Man's World*. London: Harper Collins.

Brown, A., McCrone, D. and Paterson, L. (1998), *Politics and Society in Scotland*. Basingstoke: Palgrave Macmillan.

Burke, L., Crowley, T., and Girvin, A. (eds) (2000), *The Routledge Language and Cultural Theory Reader*. London and New York: Routledge.

Burnett, F.H. (1994 [1911]), *The Secret Garden*. London: Puffin.

BIBLIOGRAPHY

Butts, D. (ed.) (1992), *Stories and Society: Children's Literature in its Social Context*. Basingstoke and London: Palgrave Macmillan.

Cadden, M. (1997), 'Home Is a Matter of Blood, Time, and Genre: Essentialism in Burnett and McKinley', *Ariel*, 28:1, 53–67.

Caine, B. (1997), *English Feminism, 1780–1980*. Oxford: Oxford University Press.

Carpenter, H. (1985), *Secret Gardens: A Study of the Golden Age of Children's Literature*. London: George Allen and Unwin.

Carroll, L., *Alice's Adventures in Wonderland* and *Through the Looking-Glass and What Alice Found There* in Gardner, M. (1970 [1960]), *The Annotated Alice*. Harmondsworth: Penguin.

Carter, J. (1999), *Talking Books: Children's Authors Talk About the Craft, Creativity and Process of Writing*. London: Routledge.

Cixous, H. (1982), 'Introduction to Lewis Carroll's *Through the Looking-Glass* and *The Hunting of the Snark*', *New Literary History*, 13:2, 231–51.

Colebrook, C. (2004), *Gender*. Hampshire: Palgrave.

Comte, F. (1994 [1988]), *The Wordsworth Dictionary of Mythology*. Ware: Wordsworth Editions.

Craig, C. (1999), *The Modern Scottish Novel: Narrative and the National Imagination*. Edinburgh: Edinburgh University Press.

Cunningham, H. (2005 [1995]), *Children and Childhood in Western Society Since 1500*. London: Longman.

—. (2006), *The Invention of Childhood*. London: BBC Books.

Davidson, P. (2005), *The Idea of North*. London: Reaktion.

Denisoff, D. (ed.) (2008), *The Nineteenth-Century Child and Consumer Culture*. Aldershot: Ashgate.

Eagleton, T. (1993 [1983]), *Literary Theory: An Introduction*. Oxford: Blackwell.

Easthope, A., and McGowan, K. (eds) (1992), *A Critical and Cultural Theory Reader*. Buckingham: Open University Press.

Eccleshare, J. (2002), *A Guide to the Harry Potter Novels*. London and New York: Continuum.

Eigner, E.M., and Worth, G.J. (eds) (1985), *Victorian Criticism of the Novel*. Cambridge: Cambridge University Press.

Elbert, M. (2008), *Enterprising Youth: Social Values and Acculturation in Nineteenth-Century American Children's Literature*. London and New York: Routledge.

Elphinstone, M. (2000) 'Fantasising Texts: Scottish Fantasy Today', www.arts.gla.ac.uk/scotlit/asls/MElphinstone.html

Foster, S., and Simmons, J. (1995), *What Katy Read: Feminist Re-Readings of 'Classic' Stories for Girls*. Basingstoke and London: Macmillan.

Fraser, L. (2002 [2000]), *An Interview With J.K. Rowling*. London: Egmont Books.

Freud, S. (1991 [1905]), *On Sexuality: Three Essays on the Theory of Sexuality and Other Works*. London: Penguin.

Froebel, F. (1899), *Education by Development: The Second Part of the Pedagogics of the Kindergarten*, tr. Josephine Jarvis. London: Edward Arnold.

Gavin, A.E., and Humphries, A.F. (eds) (2009), *Childhood in Edwardian Fiction: Worlds Enough and Time*. London and New York: Palgrave Macmillan.

Gifford, D., Dunnigan, S., and MacGillivray, A. (2002), *Scottish Literature*. Edinburgh: Edinburgh University Press.

Gilbert. S.M., and Gubar, S. (1984 [1979]), *The Madwoman in the Attic: The Woman Writer and the Nineteenth-Century Literary Imagination*. New Haven and London: Yale University Press.

Gilroy, P. (2004), *After Empire: Melancholia or Convivial Culture?* Abingdon: Routledge.

Gooderham, D. (1995), 'Children's Fantasy Literature: Toward an Anatomy', *Children's Literature in Education*, 26:3, 171–83.

Grenby, M.O. (2008), *Children's Literature*. Edinburgh: Edinburgh University Press.

Gubar, M. (2009), *Artful Dodgers: Reconceiving the Golden Age of Children's Literature*. Oxford: Oxford University Press.

Gupta, S. (2003), *Re-Reading Harry Potter*. Basingstoke: Palgrave Macmillan.

Haase, D. (ed.) (2004), *Fairy Tales and Feminism: New Approaches*. Detroit: Waynes State University Press.

Hand, N. 'Anxieties of Authorship in the *Alice* Books; or, "Sentence First – Verdict Afterwards": The Trial of Lewis Carroll' in Broadbent et al. (eds) (1994), *Researching Children's Literature – A Coming of Age?* pp. 36–43.

Hannon, P. (1998), *Fabulous Identities: Women's Fairy Tales in Seventeenth-Century France*. Amsterdam: Rodopi.

Heilman, E.E. (ed.) (2003), *Harry Potter's World: Multidisciplinary Critical Perspectives*. New York and London: Routledge Falmer.

Heywood, C. (2004 [2001]), *A History of Childhood: Children and Childhood in the West from Medieval to Modern Times*. Cambridge: Polity Press.

Hourihan, M. (1997), *Deconstructing the Hero: Literary Theory and Children's Literature*. London and New York: Routledge.

Hunt, P. (1984–85), 'Narrative Theory and Children's Literature', *Children's Literature Association Quarterly*, 9:4, 191–94.

—. (1994), *An Introduction to Children's Literature*. Oxford: Oxford University Press.

—. (2001), *Children's Literature*. Oxford: Blackwell.

Hunt, P. (ed.). (1990), *Children's Literature: The Development of Criticism*. London and New York: Routledge.

—. (1992), *Literature For Children: Contemporary Criticism*. London and New York: Routledge.

—. (1995), *Children's Literature: An Illustrated History*. Oxford: Oxford University Press.

—. (2007 [2005]), *Understanding Children's Literature*, 2nd edn. London and New York: Routledge.

Hunt, P. and Lenz, M. (2001), *Alternative Worlds in Fantasy Fiction: Ursula Le Guin, Terry Pratchett, Philip Pullman and Others*. London and New York: Continuum.

Jackson, R. (1998 [1981]), *Fantasy: The Literature of Subversion*. London and New York: Routledge.

Junko, Y. (2003), 'Uneasy Men in the Land of Oz', in McGillis, R. (ed.) (2003), *Children's Literature and the Fin de Siecle*. Connecticut and London: Praeger Press.

Kincaid, J.R. (1992), *Child-Loving: The Erotic Child and Victorian Culture*. London and New York: Routledge.

Kinglsey, C. (ed. by Alderson B.) (1995 [1863]), *The Water-Babies: A Fairy Tale for a Land-Baby*. Oxford: Oxford University Press.

Knowles, M. and Malmkjaer, K. (1996), *Language and Control in Children's Literature*. London and New York: Routledge.

Le Guin, U.K. (1980), *The Language of the Night: Essays on Fantasy and Science Fiction*. New York: Putnam.

Leitch, T. (2007), *Film Adaptation and Its Discontents*. Baltimore: The John Hopkins University Press.

Lenz, M. with Scott, C. (eds) (2005), *His Dark Materials Illuminated: Critical Essays on Philip Pullman's Trilogy*. Detroit: Wayne State University Press.

Lesnik-Oberstein, K. (1994), *Children's Literature: Criticism and the Fictional Child*. Oxford: Clarendon Press.

Lesnik-Oberstein, K. (ed.) (2004), *Children's Literature: New Approaches*. Hampshire and New York: Palgrave Macmillan.

Lewis, C.S. (1980 [1950]), *The Lion, The Witch and The Wardrobe*. London: HarperCollins.

Littlefield, H.M. (1964), '*The Wizard of Oz*: Parable on Populism', *American Quarterly*, 16:1, 47–58.

Lopez, B. (1999 [1986]), *Arctic Dreams: Imagination and Desire in a Northern Landscape*. London: The Harvill Press.

Lurie, A. (2003), *Boys and Girls Forever: Children's Classics from Cinderella to Harry Potter*. London: Vintage.

McCulloch, F. (2000), '"The Broken Telescope": Misrepresentation, *The Coral Island*' in *Children's Literature Association Quarterly*, 25:3, 137–45.

—. (2003), '"Playing Double": Performing Childhood in *Treasure Island*', *Scottish Studies Review*, 4:2, 66–81.

—. (2004), *The Fictional Role of Childhood in Victorian and Early Twentieth-Century Children's Literature*. Lampeter: Edwin Mellen Press.

—. (2007a), '"A New Home in the World": Scottish Devolution, Nomadic Writing, and Supranational Citizenship in Julie Bertagna's *Exodus* and *Zenith*, 69–96.

—. (2007b), '"Refugees Returning to their Homeland": Regaining Paradise in *His Dark Materials*' in Ousley, L. (ed.) *To See the Wizard: Politics and the Literature of Childhood*. Newcastle: Cambridge Scholars Publishing, pp.150–75.

McGavran, J.H. (1999), *Literature and the Child: Romantic Continuations, Postmodern Contestations*. Iowa City: University of Iowa Press.

McGillis, R. (1983), 'Fantasy as Adventure: Nineteenth Century Children's Fiction', *Children's Literature Association Quarterly*, 8:3, 18–22.

—. (2003), *Children's Literature and the Fin de Siecle*. Connecticut and London: Praeger Press.

Macherey, P. (2006 [1978]), *A Theory of Literary Production*. Abingdon and New York: Routledge.

Mackey, M. (1996), 'Strip Mines in the Garden: Old Stories, New Formats, and the Challenge of Change', *Children's Literature in Education*, 27:1, 3–22.

Maher, S.N. (1988), 'Recasting Crusoe: Frederick Marryat, R.M. Ballantyne and the Nineteenth-Century Robinsonade', *Children's Literature Association Quarterly*, 13:4, 169–75.

Maixner, P. (ed.) (1981), *Robert Louis Stevenson: The Critical Heritage*. London: Routledge and Kegan Paul.

Manlove, C. (2003), *From Alice to Harry Potter: Children's Fantasy in England*. Christchurch: Cybereditions.

Maybin, J. and N.J. Watson (eds) (2009), *Children's Literature: Approaches and Territories*. Basingstoke: Palgrave Macmillan.

Montgomery, H., and Watson, N.J. (eds) (2009), *Children's Literature: Classic Texts and Contemporary Trends*. Basingstoke: Palgrave Macmillan.

Murdoch, I. (1978), *The Fire and the Sun: Why Plato Banished the Artists*. Oxford: Oxford University Press.

Murray, G.S. (1998), *American Children's Literature and the Construction of Childhood*. Michigan: Twayne Publishers.

Murray, H. (1985), 'Frances Hodgson Burnett's *The Secret Garden*: The Organ(ic)ized World', in P. Nodelman (ed.), *Touchstones: Reflections on the Best in Children's Literature, Vol.1*. West Lafayette: Children's Literature Association, Purdue University, 30–42.

Natov, R. (2006 [2003]), *The Poetics of Childhood*. London and New York: Routledge.

Nelson, C. (1991), *Boys Will be Girls: The Feminine Ethic and British Children's Fiction, 1857–1917*. New Jersey: Rutgers University Press.

Nikolajeva, M. (2003), '*Harry Potter* – A Return to the Romantic Hero', Heilman, E.E. (ed.) (2003), *Harry Potter's World: Multidisciplinary Critical Perspectives*. New York and London: Routledge Falmer.

Nodelman, P. (1985), 'The Case of Children's Fiction: or the Impossibility of Jacqueline Rose', *Children's Literature Association Quarterly*, 10:3, 98–100.

O'Malley, J. (2007 [1994]), *Marx: Early Political Writings*. Cambridge: Cambridge University Press.

Opie, P. and Opie I. (2001 [1959]), *The Lore and Language of Schoolchildren*. New York: New York Review Books.

Opie, P. and Opie I. (eds) (1997 [1951]), *The Oxford Dictionary of Nursery Rhymes*. Oxford: Oxford University Press.

Ousley, L. (ed.) (2007), *To See the Wizard: Politics and the Literature of Childhood*. Newcastle: Cambridge Scholars Publishing.

Phillips, J. (1993), 'The Mem Sahib, the Worthy, the Rajah and His Minions: Some Reflections on the Class Politics of *The Secret Garden*', *The Lion and the Unicorn*, 17:2, 169–94.

Postman, N. (1994 [1982]), *The Disappearance of Childhood*. New York: Vintage Books.

Pullman, P. (1998a [1995]), *Northern Lights*. London and New York: Scholastic.

—. (1998b [1997]), *The Subtle Knife*. London and New York: Scholastic.

—. (2001 [2000]), *The Amber Spyglass*. London and New York: Scholastic.

Rackin, D. (1987), 'Love and Death in Carroll's *Alices*' in Bloom, H. (ed.), *Modern Critical Views: Lewis Carroll*. New York and Philadelphia: Chelsea House Publishers.

Reynolds, K. (1990), *Girls Only? Gender and Popular Children's Fiction in Britain, 1880–1910*. London and New York: Harvester Wheatsheaf.

—. (1994), *Children's Literature in the 1890s and the 1990s*. Plymouth: Northcote House.

—. (2005), *Modern Children's Literature: An Introduction*. London and New York: Palgrave Macmillan.

—. (2007), *Radical Children's Literature: Future Visions and Aesthetic Transformations in Juvenile Fiction*. London and New York: Palgrave Macmillan.

Riach, A. (1996), '*Treasure Island* and Time', *Children's Literature in Education*, 27:3, 181–93.

Rose, J. (1994 [1984]), *The Case of Peter Pan; Or the Impossibility of Children's Fiction*. Basingstoke and London: Macmillan.

Rousseau, J.J. (1991 [1762]), *Emile: Or on Education*, tr. Allan Bloom. London: Penguin.

Rowling, J.K. (1997), *Harry Potter and the Philosopher's Stone*. London: Bloomsbury.

—. (1998), *Harry Potter and the Chamber of Secrets*. London: Bloomsbury.

—. (1999), *Harry Potter and the Prisoner of Azkaban*. London: Bloomsbury.

—. (2000), *Harry Potter and the Goblet of Fire*. London: Bloomsbury.

—. (2003), *Harry Potter and the Order of the Phoenix*. London: Bloomsbury.

—. (2005), *Harry Potter and the Half-Blood Prince*. London: Bloomsbury.

—. (2007), *Harry Potter and the Deathly Hallows*. London: Bloomsbury.

Royle, N. (2003), *The Uncanny*. Manchester: Manchester University Press.

Rudd, D. (2000), *Enid Blyton and the Mystery of Children's Literature*. Basingstoke and New York: Palgrave Macmillan.

—. 'Theorising and Theories: How Does Children's Literature Exist?', in Hunt, P. (ed.) (2007 [2005]), *Understanding Children's Literature*, 2nd edn. London and New York: Routledge.

Rudd, D. (ed.) (2010), *The Routledge Companion to Children's Literature*. London and New York: Routledge.

Russell, M.H. (2005), '"Eve, Again! Mother Eve!": Pullman's Eve Variations', in Lenz, M., with Scott, C. (eds) (2005), *His Dark Materials Illuminated: Critical Essays on Philip Pullman's Trilogy*. Detroit: Wayne State University Press.

Rustin, M. and Rustin, M. (2001), *Narratives of Love and Loss: Studies in Modern Children's Fiction*. London and New York: Karnac.

Sandison, A. (1996), *Robert Louis Stevenson and the Appearance of Modernism: A Future Feeling.* London: Macmillan.

Seifert, L.C. (1996), *Fairy Tales, Sexuality, and Gender in France, 1690–1715.* Cambridge: Cambridge University Press.

Sherman, C. (1987), 'The Princess and the Wizard: The Fantasy Worlds of Ursula K. LeGuin and George MacDonald', *Children's Literature Association Quarterly,* 12:1, 24–7.

Shires, L.M. (1988), 'Fantasy, Nonsense, Parody, and the Status of the Real: The Example of Lewis Carroll', *Victorian Poetry,* 26:3, 267–83.

Showalter, E. (1982 1978]), *A Literature of Their Own.* London: Virago.

Smith, S. (2001), *J.K. Rowling: A Biography.* London: Michael O'Mara Books.

Squires, C. (2003), *Philip Pullman's His Dark Materials Trilogy: A Reader's Guide.* London and New York: Continuum.

Stam, R. and Raengo, A. (eds) (2005), *Literature and Film: A Guide to the Theory and Practice of Film Adaptation.* Oxford: Blackwell.

Stephens, J. (1992), *Language and Ideology in Children's Fiction.* London and New York: Longman.

Stevenson, R.L. (1883), *Treasure Island* (ed. and intro. Emma Letley [1985]). Oxford: Oxford University Press.

Stone, L. (1990 [1977]), *The Family, Sex and Marriage in England 1500–1800.* London: Penguin.

Styles, M., Bearne, E. and Watson, V. (eds) (1996), *Voices Off: Texts, Contexts and Readers.* London: Cassell.

Sutherland, R.D. (1985), 'Hidden Persuaders: Political Ideologies in Literature for Children', *Children's Literature in Education,* 16:3, 143–57.

Tatar, M. (ed.) (1999), *The Classic Fairy Tales.* New York and London: W.W. Norton and Co.

Thacker, D. C., and Webb, J. (2002), *Introducing Children's Literature: From Romanticism to Postmodernism.* London and New York: Routledge.

Todorov, T. (1975 [1970]), *The Fantastic: A Structural Approach to a Literary Genre.* New York: Cornell University Press.

Touponce, W.F. (1995–96), 'Children's Literature and the Pleasures of the Text', *Children's Literature Association Quarterly,* 20:4, 175–81.

Townsend, J.R. (1974 [1965]), *Written For Children: An Outline of English-Language Children's Literature.* Harmondsworth: Penguin.

Wall, B. (1991), *The Narrator's Voice: The Dilemma of Children's Fiction.* London: Macmillan.

Walsh, C. (2003), 'From "Capping" to Intercision: Metaphors/Metonyms of Mind Control in the Young Adult Fiction of John Christopher and Philip Pullman', *Language and Literature,* 12:3, 233–51.

Warner, M. (1995 [1994]), *From the Beast to the Blonde: On Fairy Tales and Their Tellers.* London: Vintage.

West, M.I. (1992), 'The Dorothys of Oz: A Heroine's Unmaking', in Butts, D. (ed.), *Stories and Society: Children's Literature in its Social Context.* Basingstoke and London: Palgrave Macmillan.

Wood, N. (2009 [2001], 'Obedience, Disobedience, and Storytelling in C.S. Lewis and Philip Pullman', in Montgomery, H., and Watson, N.J. (eds) (2009), *Children's Literature: Classic Texts and Contemporary Trends*. Basingstoke: Palgrave Macmillan.

Wullschlager, J. (2001), *Inventing Wonderland: The Lives of Lewis Carroll, Edward Lear, J.M. Barrie, Kenneth Grahame and A.A. Milne*. London: Methuen.

Zipes, J. (1989) [1986], *Don't Bet on the Prince: Contemporary Feminist Fairy Tales in North America and England*. New York and London: Routledge.

—. (1991[1983]), *Fairy Tales and the Art of Subversion: The Classical Genre for Children and the Process of Civilization*. New York and London: Routledge.

—. (1994), *Fairy Tale as Myth/Myth as Fairy Tale*. Kentucky: University of Kentucky Press.

—. (2002 [2001]), *Sticks and Stones: The Troublesome Success of Children's Literature from Slovenly Peter to Harry Potter*. New York and London: Routledge.

The Holy Bible, Authorized King James Version. London: Oxford University Press.

WEB RESOURCES

http://digital.nls.uk/rlstevenson/
www.endicott-studio.com/rdrm/forconte.html
http://lewiscarrollsociety.org.uk/
http://geology.wcupa.edu/mgagne/ess362/homework/constellations/lyra.htm
http://myweb.dal.ca/barkerb/fairies/resource.html
http://news.bbc.co.uk/1/hi/despatches/americas/25908.stm
http://people.ucalgary.ca/~dkbrown/
http://scholar.lib.vt.edu/ejournals/ALAN/
http://thewizardofoz.info/
http://webexhibits.org/causesofcolor/4C.html
http://virtual.finland.fi/finfo/english/aurora_borealis.html
http://voc.ucsb.edu
www.answers.com/topic/north-pole
www.childlitassn.org/
www.delanet.com/~ftise/pullman.html
www.english.heacademy.ac.uk
www.environmentalrefugee.org/facts.html#
www.intute.ac.uk/humanities
www.ipl.org/div/pf/entry/48473
www.irscl.ac.uk
www.jkrowling.com/
www.juliebertagna.com/
www.juliebertagna.com/start.html

BIBLIOGRAPHY

www.lewiscarroll.org/
www.lib.latrobe.edu.au/ojs/index.php/tlg
www.philip-pullman.com/
www.robert-louis-stevenson.org.uk
www.victorianweb.org/

INDEX

INDEX